A Photo

SEASHORE
OF AUSTRALIA

Keith Davey

First published in Australia in 1998 by
New Holland Publishers (Australia) Pty Ltd
Sydney • London • Cape Town

14 Aquatic Drive Frenchs Forest
NSW 2086 Australia
24 Nutford Place London
W1H 6DQ United Kingdom
80 McKenzie Street Cape Town
8001 South Africa

National Library of Australia
  Cataloguing-in-Publication data

  Davey, Keith, 1944–
  A photographic guide to seashore life of Australia.
  Includes index.

  ISBN 1 86436 303 7

  1. Marine animals — Australia — Identification. 2. Marine
  animals — Australia — Pictorial works. 3. Marine plants —
  Australia — Identification. 4. Marine plants — Australia —
  Pictorial works I. Title.

  578.770994

Publishing General Manager: Jane Hazell
Publisher: Averill Chase
Project Manager: Fiona Doig
Scientific Consultant: Phil Colman
Edited by Robyn Flemming and Lynn Cole
Page layout by DiZign
Reproduction by cmyk pre-press, Cape Town
Printed and bound by Tien Wah Press (Pte) Ltd
Front Cover Photo: Waratah Anemone by Rudie Kuiter.
Back Cover Photo: Orange-clawed Fiddler Crab by Keith Davey.
Spine Photo: Tulip Shell by Keith Davey,

Contents

Introduction	4
Wave energy	4
Rocky shores	4
Zonation	5
Biogeographic zones	7
How to use this book	8
Biology	9
Biological factors	11
Classification	12
External features of seashore organisms	16
Key to symbols	18
Safety and field hints	19
Species accounts	
Algae	20
Sponges	30
Anemones	31
Worms	37
Barnacles	40
Slaters	45
Crabs	46
Chitons	69
Abalone	74
Limpet	75
Gastropods	86
Siphon Shell	117
Sea Hares	120
Bivalves	122
Sea Stars	128
Urchins	133
Holothorian	135
Cunjevoi	136
Gulls	137
Glossary	138
Further reading	141
Index	142

Introduction

Australia has a coastline length of about 37,000km and its coasts may be divided into four major groupings: rock, mainland beach, barrier beach and tidal plain.

Rocky coasts These all have cliffs of varying degrees of slope and ruggedness. They occur in southern and north-western Australia. The associated beaches are of minor importance.

Mainland beach coasts Extensive ocean beaches are dominant, bounded by rocky headlands, reefs and shore platforms. Large intertidal platforms, swashed over by waves, are excellent habitats for intertidal animals and algae.

Barrier beach coasts These occur where beaches have formed off rocky promontories, partially enclosing lagoons and estuaries between themselves and the old shore. Common on the east coast between Bass Strait and the Tropic of Capricorn, eastern SA and south of Perth. Small barrier shores occur in tropical north-eastern Queensland and some Northern Territory coasts.

Tidal plain coasts Mangroves and salt marsh are present and sometimes also a fringing coral reef. Extensive between North West Cape and Port Hedland and in the tropical and temperate gulfs.

Wave energy

Spray and mist from strong waves can moisten rock surfaces far above the highest tide levels. ***Littorina*** and ***Nodilittorina*** species are found here. Mudflats form only where there are quiet waters.

Southern Australia From Fraser Island, south-eastern Queensland, around the southern shores to Shark Bay in WA, the coast is subjected to high-energy waves from the mid-latitude storm belt of the Southern Ocean and Tasman Sea (40–60°S). Here, there are no tidal flats. Mudflats form only in estuaries and sheltered inlets protected from ocean swell.

Northern Australia In the tropics, wave energy is low, except for occasional cyclones. Central and north-eastern Queensland coasts are sheltered by the Great Barrier Reef. Fine sediment is not washed out to sea, so most coastlines and creatures are covered with a layer of mud. Mangrove forests are extremely important here.

In the tropics, shores extend out from a low-lying mainland, with virtually no cliffs. There is a succession of sandy, shell-grit and coral-rubble beaches, mudflats and mangroves. There are a few rocky reefs and low outcrops of weathered sandstone beach rock. Scattered boulders lie everywhere. Usually there is an extensive fringing reef. In tropical Australia there is a food chain that is plankton- and detritus-driven, not algae-driven as along the southern shores.

Rocky shores

Between the beaches are the rocky headlands. Some dip steeply into the ocean, while others are more gently sloping. Some are strongly contorted and broken, while others form horizontal platforms and reefs. Each rocky headland type has a range of habitats and microhabitats.

Granite shores Large granite domes form a distinctive shoreline in Tasmania, on some South Australian capes and in south-western Australia. Locally known as 'turtle-backs', these domes plunge into the sea with no associated reefs or platforms. Only a narrow band of almost vertical rock is intertidal. Here animals and algae are hardy, because they are subjected to the full force of huge cold-water waves from the Southern Ocean.

Basalt shores Basalt shores erode to form extensive low-ridged rock platforms backed by steep cliffs, such as those in central Victoria along the Great Coast Road. Gutters, channels and small protected embayments are excellent shelters for intertidal creatures such as mussels, anemones, limpets and top shells, and a great variety of algal species. Rocky basalt shores and sandy beaches alternate along the shore.

Limestone shores Limestone or sand-rock shores are found in parts of Victoria and SA and extensively in WA and the Northern Territory. They form distinctive eroded landscapes, becoming twisted and contorted as they are eaten away by weathering and wave power. These form long, wide horizontal platforms and reefs backed by steep cliffs. Horizontal platforms are uncovered at low tide, while lower limestone reefs are swashed over by waves, even when the tide is at its lowest. Limestone shores, with their pitted and broken surfaces, deep gutters and channels, are excellent habitats for many intertidal species.

Sandstone shores Between Newcastle and Kiama, NSW, vast intertidal wavecut platforms form extensive horizontal surfaces that suit intertidal algae and creatures. The waves dissipate most of their energy as they roll across the wide expanse of platform. Gutters, cracks and crannies cut deep across the platform. In rock pools and under boulders lying on rock or sand, numerous protected microhabitats occur. Algae clumps also form a protective cover.

Metamorphic rock shores There are highly contorted and fractured metamorphic rock coasts where steeply dipping strata has weathered to form an angular and dissected landscape. These form protective cracks, crannies, overhangs and wave-swashed channels in which intertidal animals can shelter.

Boulder shores Here there are numerous, round to egg-shaped boulders of various sizes. On high-energy shores life can be precarious, but in more sheltered locations the boulder spaces form a particularly good environment for a wide range of animals that hide.

Zonation

On a slope, each type of organism has a preferred habitat range, with an upper and a lower limit determined by different environmental and biological factors. Distinct parallel bands of species can occur across rocky shores, which is called intertidal zonation.

Sandy shore zonation On high-energy sandy beaches the sand is coarse and generally slopes away into the water. These beaches have the lowest number of animals. Protected beaches have fine sand, which, if supported by water, is easy to penetrate and remains moist. Here a large range of very small animals move among sand particles in suspension. In Australia we know very little about these microscopic animals. Other larger animals are the **Ocean Beach Surf Crab** (*Ovalipes australiensis*), **Two-spined Burrowing Sand Crab** (*Matuta planipes*) as well as **Pipis** (*Plebidonax deltoides*), several species of beachworms, isopods and amphipods (sand-hoppers),which are often found under torn-off algae fronds. No large algae occur here, only microscopic algae.

High on a sandy shore are the **Ocypode crabs** (the eastern *Ocypode cordimana* and western *Ocypode convexa*), the related **Sand Bubbler Crab** (*Scopimera inflata*) and the **Burrowing Shore Crab** (*Leptograpsus octodentatus*) of the southern shores.

Estuarine shore zonation Close to an estuary or river mouth, the shore is usually sand. Because wave energy is not as strong as along the open ocean, the sand is usually packed down more firmly. This is not a suitable habitat for intertidal animals.

Moving away from the entrance, wave energy decreases and the percentage of mud increases. Here extensive seagrass beds occur. Many intertidal and estuarine-preferring species are associated with seagrasses and the rich flats. Further into the embayment, muddy shores increase in importance, fringed by mangrove forest and backed by extensive salt-marsh flats, covered only by the highest tides. Where a river enters an estuary, the water becomes brackish, so oysters, mud whelks and polychaete worms become dominant.

All these habitats have their own specialised creatures and plant forms which, when occurring on a shore, lie in parallel bands. The gentler the slope, the broader the habitat band. But here most species are not attached to the substrate, so it is more like a zonation of habitats and their associated organisms.

Rocky shore zonation On rocky shores, the horizontal banding of creatures is generally obvious and is called intertidal zonation. Researchers have used the varying lunar-month tide levels and/or indicator species to define these levels. Some terminology is complex and uses descriptions such as infralittoral, high midlittoral, high-water spring and high-water neap tides, upper and lower barnacle zones and cunjevoi zone.

In this book a generalised scheme is adopted based on assumed tidal levels for any Australian shore.

Splash fringe level The level immediately above the highest tide level reached in any month. It may be wetted by spray and mist. On some wave-smashed rugged shores it may extend a few hundred metres up the shore or up a cliff face. On calm-water shores, this zone will not exist.

High-tide level The upper part of this level is covered by the tide for only up to a few hours each day. The dominant sessile organisms are high-shore barnacles. Below these are the semi-mobile molluscs, such as acmaeid limpets, patelloid limpets, siphon shells, chitons, top shells, conniwinks and some nerites.

Mid-tide level Along many south-eastern shores, there is a characteristic band of hard, white, limy *Galeolaria* tube-worms which, in some locations, occur in dense colonies. Many intertidal organisms are adapted to living in the microhabitat provided by thick tube-worm colonies. This level is covered and uncovered for about an equal time each tide cycle.

Low-tide level This cunjevoi region is uncovered for only a few hours each tidal cycle and is the favoured habitat of a large range of intertidal species. Most species in this book are found at this level, and include anemones, sea stars, urchins, chitons, tritons, whelks, limpets, barnacles and crabs. Some algal species occur in moist crevices, gutters and rock pools.

Low fringe level Here, low tide oscillates during a lunar month, and at low tide this level is wetted and exposed during each wave. Most creatures and algae here are fully marine and are not really adapted to spending some time exposed. Some carnivores move into the intertidal region to eat easily captured attached prey, such as barnacles, cunjevoi and slow-moving limpets. Most algal species occur here.

Marine or sub-tidal level Species found here are not adapted to spending any of their life cycle in the intertidal zone. Some come in at high tide as predators of intertidal species. Many carnivorous fish and decapod crabs fit this category. A large range of algae are found here.

	Littorinids
Splash Fringe Level	High-shore
High-Tide Level	Barnacles
Mid-Tide Level	Limpets, Top Shells
	Conniwinks, Siphon Shells
Low-Tide Level	Galeolaria, Chitons, Seastars
Low Fringe Level	Shore Crabs, Balanus Barnacles
Marine	Red, Green and Brown Algae
	Cunjevoi, Sponges, Urchins, Holothurians
	Polychaete Worms, Whelks, Tritons, Turbans

Biogeographic zones

Australia is divided into a northern tropical region and a southern temperate region. Across northern Australia is an Eastern Tropical Zone and a Western Tropical Zone. Southern Australia is divided into an Eastern Warm Temperate Zone, a Western Warm Temperate Zone and a more southerly Cool Temperate Zone.

Some zones have sharp boundaries, such as near Fraser Island, Queensland, while others merge gradually from one type to the other, such as near Geraldton and Shark Bay in WA. The Cold Temperate Zone overlaps both the Eastern Warm Temperate Zone and the Western Warm Temperate Zone. So along southern Victorian shores there are creatures that are typically eastern warm temperate species, while others are typically cool temperate species, usually occupying different (but sometimes the same) habitats. Possibly one group is more dominant in summer, while the other is more dominant in winter.

Eastern tropical zone This zone extends along north-eastern Queensland from Cape York to Fraser Island. Most of it is protected by the offshore Great Barrier Reef, which forms an almost estuary-like environment with lots of muddy shores and long regions of sand, shell and coral rubble beaches, and with relatively few rocky headlands and platforms.

Eastern warm temperate zone This runs from Fraser Island, southern Queensland, to Cape Otway in Victoria, including south-eastern Queensland, NSW, eastern Victoria and north-eastern Tasmania. Most are long sandy beaches bounded by rocky headlands, but between Newcastle and Kiama are large sandstone horizontal platforms. Some headlands and rocky regions are granitic, basaltic or metamorphic, with some limestone coasts along southern Victoria.

Cool temperate zone This zone runs from Bermagui, NSW, around Tasmania, across Victoria into SA, overlapping other zones. The species that prefer cooler waters inhabit this zone and are typically found in regions of cold water upwelling near Eden in NSW, Robe in SA and around Tasmania.

Western warm temperate zone This zone is from Cape Otway, Victoria, across SA, around south-western Australia, gradually fading out at Shark Bay, central coast of WA. It includes north-west Tasmania. There are lots of limestone shores, with platforms and reefs, with some long sandy beaches. The steep rounded headlands, such as those in Tasmania and south-western Australia, are granite 'turtle-back' domes. There are also some basalt and metamorphic rocky headland and shores.

Western tropical zone This runs from Geraldton, WA, across northern Australia to Cape York in Queensland. Mostly it consists of long sandy, or sand-shell-coral rubble to sand-mud beaches or tidal plain muddy shores. There are some regions of coarse sandstone-limestone 'sand-rock' shores. True rocky shores are found only in the Kimberley and other isolated areas.

Biogeographic Zones around Australia

How to use this book

This book was designed as a true field guide. If you walk down any coastal shore around Australia at low tide, you should be able to identify many animals and algae species sighted by using the photographs in this book. The species selected are the most common and easily found, rather than hard-to-find or rare forms.

Look at the side-on shape of the animal or plant to be identified and use the page silhouettes as a guide to the group in which the unknown species might be located. Remember that there may be quite a bit of variation in form and coloration, which will make your task more difficult. Erosion, weathering and algal growths can discolour and distort mollusc shells. Some creatures grow taller, larger and stronger in areas of strong wave battering than do others in more sheltered areas.

Also, a few species look dissimilar in different parts of their range. If so, it is usually mentioned in the description, and sometimes photos of the different forms have been included. All measurements are the maximum length, height or diameter, whichever is the largest, usually in millimetres.

No other field guide of Australian shore life has attempted to plot distribution ranges. Many word descriptions in existing texts and research papers are quite vague — for example, 'extends to Western Australia'. The Western Australian coastline is almost one-third that of Australia, so this word description is far from useful, but is the best that exists. If distribution maps are found to be inaccurate, please advise the publisher, so that the maps can be amended in future editions.

Read through the classification descriptions as well. This section contains information relevant to the whole group and may make the task of locating a species easier. If you have found a species not described in this book, check in the Further Reading section on page 141 for other useful sources of information.

Biology

The environment on rocky ocean shores is hazardous. At high tide, it may be battered by the waves and predators are common. At low tide, algae and animals are baked by the sun or drenched by fresh water from rain. Because high-tide levels vary from day to day and during the month, some fixed creatures high on the shore may not be wetted for days, or even weeks, at a time. Yet they survive and thrive in a habitat that appears so inhospitable.

Environmental factors Every animal and algae on a shore is affected by a range of environmental and biological factors. Each organism has the capacity to cope with a particular range within those factors. If a situation occurs that overly stresses an organism, it may cope for a short while but will ultimately die. If its offspring are not capable of existing in the new environment, then the species will be unable to remain established on that shore.

Latitude Australia is half tropical and half temperate. Most marine and shore organisms are either northern or southern in their distribution patterns. There are some exceptions to this, with some endemic eastern and endemic western species. There also appears to be a major sharp divide near Fraser Island off the coast of Queensland and a more diffuse overlap in the Geraldton–Shark Bay region of WA.

Currents For a population of organisms to be maintained on any given shore, there must be an overall circular pattern to the currents over time. If the organism's offspring are tiny plankton, this is necessary for them to be delivered back to that particular shore. If not, the species must become extinct on that shore.

The following description of Australian currents is greatly simplified, and it varies throughout the seasons. Generally, south of Australia, in the Southern Ocean, the dominating current is the prevailing West Wind Drift, which flows from west to east. Along eastern Australia, the dominant current is the warm, southward-flowing East Australian Current, which meets Australia near the southern Great Barrier Reef and flows down the NSW coast, swinging away near Eden. The western WA shores have a south to north current in summer but this is more variable in winter. Across southern Australia, including south-west Australia, the currents are complex, flowing westward in summer from Tasmania to Cape Leeuwin in WA, and more-or-less eastward in winter. In Bass Strait, the circulation of water is very complex.

Wind effects Deep ocean swells tend to be bigger and more powerful along southern shores. Strong daily winds create waves on top of the swell. Southern, south-eastern and south-western Australia are continually barraged by waves as they come ashore. In northern Australia, wave-energy levels are dissipated by a number of geographic effects. Australia bulges near Fraser Island in the east and North West Cape in the west, so northern shores run in the same direction as the southern waves approach. Also, most of Queensland's coast is protected in an estuary-like situation behind the Great Barrier Reef.

Wave strength, aspect and battering Water is not static. Every rock surface, sandy shore and mud shore is affected by the seawater that surges against it. Sometimes this may be a gentle surge but at other times rocks and beach are pounded by storm waves. The creatures on the surface of a boulder facing the battering waves have a much rougher time than those on the rear, in the wave shadow. This determines the type of species found on an individual boulder or rock face. Surf barnacles occur on the ocean face, while other barnacles prefer a more protected habitat. Interestingly, many species prefer living on the ocean face in regions of smashing water and swift currents because this is where there is abundant planktonic and detritus food.

Tide effects Along eastern and western Australian shores there are two high and two low tides every 24 hours. In south-eastern Australia, the difference between high and low tide is up to 2m. In south-western Australia, this difference is less than 1m. In north-western Australia, there is a 7m tidal range at Broome. In South Australia the tides are more problematic. The tides of the Indian Ocean and the Pacific Ocean sometimes cancel each other out, so that there is only one high tide and one low tide every 24 hours. Occasionally, the water level remains stationary for days at a time in a 'dodge tide'. If this occurs in the hot, searing summer months, all creatures on the upper shore levels perish.

Desiccation and air temperature Intertidal animals that occur above low-tide level have differing abilities to cope with being dried out by the sun. Some molluscs use a muscular foot to clamp down on to the rock, holding in moisture. Other molluscs have operculums, which are lids that accurately fit their shell aperture, holding in precious water. Most creatures that are able to move seek shelter from the sun under rocks or algae fronds, or in crevices, burrows or rock pools. Desiccation is probably the major environmental problem that must be solved by intertidal organisms.

Substrate Different species are adapted to rocky, sandy or muddy shores. But even on rocky shores there are subtle differences in the grain structure of the rock, its smoothness, indentations, cracks or gutters. One favourite habitat is under boulders. It makes a great difference to the type and number of species whether the boulder is situated on bare rock, on sand, in mud, or surrounded by thick algae against other boulders. Boulder fields situated in muddy sand in swift-flowing water with an abundance of algae is an environment that is usually rich in different intertidal species.

Turbidity Waters along southern shores are normally quite clear. However, in northern Australian embayments, especially where large freshwater rivers enter the sea, turbid waters are thick with sediment. This suits creatures such as some nerites and crabs, but excludes others.

Salinity Salinity is not a problem on a shore covered each day by the waves, but it is a critical factor in high-shore rock pools. Many low-shore animals and algae may occur higher on a shore protected inside a permanently moist rock pool. Some rock pools are not often refreshed by seawater and are continually being dried out by the sun. Here salinity reaches levels far saltier than seawater, and the pools become ecological deserts. You may find the remains of shore crabs or bleached mollusc shells. One species of mosquito larvae thrives in these super-saline pools.

Salinity becomes important in river estuaries, where freshwater is entering, or embayments or lagoons, where water is being evaporated. In northern Australia, certain species of mangrove cannot grow on shores with a higher than normal salinity.

Biological factors

Oxygen and respiration Most sea creatures use their gills to obtain their oxygen and to release poisonous carbon dioxide into water as it flows over them. Some animals use gills to filter detritus and planktonic food out of the water. But gills will function only if they are immersed in water. So how do high-shore creatures continue to respire when the tide does not reach them, sometimes for days at a time? They can do so only if they keep their gills moist. Crabs have a gill chamber that can hold water. Molluscs can seal water inside their shell by an operculum, or by clamping down onto the rock surface.

Food and predation For an organism to grow and flourish, it must consume sufficient food to sustain it. At the first trophic level, algae absorb nutrients through their fronds from the surrounding water and create energy by the fixation of carbon by means of photosynthesis. Algae do not take in nutrients through their holdfasts.

At the second trophic level are the algae grazers. Some animals eat algae fronds and others micro-algae, scraped off moist rock surfaces. Also included at the second level are the filter feeders, sifting plankton and detritus out of water through various net-like structures such as cirri or gills, and deposit feeders eating mud and sand to extract organic matter.

At the third trophic level are many animals that are first-level carnivores, capturing and eating other organisms. Predatory molluscs are an example. The second-level carnivores include flesh-eating fish, mollusc-eating birds and humans. For animals in a marine environment there are many feeding types, including grazers, browsers, suspension feeders, deposit feeders, carnivores and omnivores.

Excretion Getting rid of waste products is important to the survival of all animals. Sea creatures, which are submerged for long periods of time, use the water swirling around them to carry away the waste products of digestive processes.

Reproduction By far the most important way creatures distribute offspring to suitable new sites is by casting their fertilised eggs or juveniles adrift as plankton into water currents. Most intertidal female animals produce hundreds, if not thousands, of eggs. Most will not survive to adulthood, but are an excellent food supply for some other animal. A planktonic development pattern is common in most cnidaria, echinoderms, molluscs, barnacles, decapod crabs and ascidians. The important issue is whether the currents will return the plankton to a suitable site for juveniles to settle and grow to become reproductively mature adults.

Behaviour The environment impinges on the daily life of each organism on the shore. How they react to that environment affects their chances of survival. Most creatures have behaviour patterns locked away in their nervous systems, so that they act appropriately when reacting to an environmental stimulus. Animals actively move toward a favourable stimulus and actively avoid unfavourable stimuli. Animals select sheltering places, hunt down desirable food, avoid harmful situations, select suitable mates to produce fertile gametes, and avoid predators. The way an animal behaves has a major effect on its continued existence.

Classification

Researchers use a classification system called taxonomy in order to group organisms. This system provides order, showing the similarities between different organisms as well as their evolutionary relationships. The broadest category is that of Kingdom (this book covers plants and animals), then this is broken down into phylum, then class, order, family, genus and, finally, species.

 The major groups included in this book are described here. Fish are excluded as most visit shores only during high tide.

 Reading the following broad descriptions can help give a general idea of the shape and various body parts to look out for in determining the group to which an organism belongs, making it easier to look up a species.

PLANTS

Phylum Chlorophyta: Green Algae
All marine algae are more commonly known as seaweed or kelp. Green algae get their colour from photosynthetic chlorophyll pigments. They have a variety of shapes including hair-like filaments, flat sheets, cylinders, strings of beads or spheres. They are common in the intertidal zones and in shallow water as well as in freshwater habitats, where light is plentiful. See pages 20–22.

Phylum Phaeophyta: Brown Algae
In the brown algae, additional pigments mask the green chlorophylls. They come in a wide variety of forms and contain the largest, longest and most conspicuous seaweeds found on rocky ocean shores and are a common feature of the low-shore fringe and shallow sub-tidal zones. Some brown kelps from southern Australian waters are the fastest growing of all plants. See pages 23–27.

Phylum Rhodophyta: Red Algae
These have various shades of red due to additional red protein pigments. These pigments allow the red algae to grow at far greater depths than the green and brown algaes; they occur down to 200m. Red algae have a wide variety of forms, including encrusting, string-like, tube-like, filamentous and flat sheets. The colour is not uniform and some species are purple, mauve, orange or even yellow. They rarely dominate reef communities, preferring deeper water. See pages 28–29.

ANIMALS

Phylum Porifera: Sponges
Sponges are the simplest multicellular animals. Filter-feeders, they usually or often attach to hard substrate where water movement is strong. The body wall has many small pores. Inflowing water supplies the sponge with unicellular algae and bacteria as food, provides oxygen and removes carbon dioxide in gas exchange, as well as removing excretory products and reproductive gametes. See page 30.

Phylum Cnidaria: Anemones, Corals and Hydroids
CLASS ANTHOZOA: SEA ANEMONES, SOFT AND HARD CORALS
Cnidarians all have a life cycle of two forms: a free-swimming jellyfish medusa stage and an attached polyp stage. Body-shape is radially symmetrical with the mouth surrounded by rings of tentacles. They all have stinging cells (poison-bearing nematocyst barbs) to harpoon and immobilise prey. See pages 31–36.

CLASS HYDROZOA: HYDROIDS
The By-the-wind Sailer (*Velella velella*) consists of a floating disc, a thin S-shaped sail on top and food-capturing nematocyst threads below. This is not a single creature but a whole colony of individual organisms that live, feed and float together. See page 34.

Phylum Annelida: Segmented Worms
CLASS POLYCHAETA: BRISTLEWORMS
The largest class of annelid worms, most are marine, with a diverse range of forms and lifestyles. Long, multi-segmented bodies have paddle-shaped parapodia along the sides, each one tipped with spines called setae. There are two groups — the free-moving Errantia and tube-living Sedentaria. Many are active carnivores and some have strong, chitinous jaws. See pages 37–39.

Phylum Sipuncula: Peanut Worms
Unsegmented, cylindrical and worm-like, these animals have a fat trunk section that extends into an eversible 'trunk-like' proboscis, with a mouth at the end. They excavate burrows under boulders lying in mud, or they bore into soft sand-rock. Peanut worms feed on organic matter that they extract from sand and mud. See page 39.

Phylum Arthropoda: Barnacles and Crustaceans

CLASS CIRRIPEDIA: BARNACLES

Barnacles are usually fixed to rock. The larvae go through several distinct swimming stages before settling into place. Adult rock barnacles are protected by four, six or eight calcareous plates, forming a volcano-like cover. The entrance is covered by another two plates. When feeding, these open and basket-like cirri limbs wave through water and direct food into the mouth. See pages 40–44.

CLASS MALACOSTRACA: PILL BUGS, SHRIMPS AND CRABS

Woodlice, Pill Bugs and Slaters form a large group of crustaceans. They are flattened top to bottom and, lacking a carapace, they have first, and sometimes second, thorax segments fused onto the head. Their gills are near the abdominal pleopods. The first pair of antennae are not forked. The first two pairs of legs are usually not clawed. See page 45.

    Decapods belong to a group that includes shrimps, prawns, lobsters, yabbies, hermit crabs, half-crabs and true crabs. All are covered with a large, hard carapace. With 10 thoracic limbs, the first pair are strong chelipeds, while the last four pairs are for walking. In swimming crabs, the last pair are paddle-shaped for digging and swimming. True crabs have a very short abdomen, which is flattened and folded tightly underneath the carapace; those of females are wider than males. Eggs attach to female pleopods under her abdomen. When the young hatch, they swim freely as plankton for a few weeks before settling. See pages 46–68.

Phylum Mollusca: Molluscs

CLASS POLYPLACOPHORA: CHITONS

These are elliptical, flattened, bilaterally symmetrical molluscs with a shell divided into eight tile-like, articulating plates, all enclosed by a strong girdle. Chitons can flex the body to fasten onto irregular rocky surfaces. They feed on encrusting algae, bryozoans and sponges by scraping them off with a long radula tongue. See pages 69–73.

CLASS GASTROPODA: GASTROPODS

This group includes sea snails, land snails, slugs, sea hares, limpets, abalones, whelks and cones. They are soft-bodied animals with a head, foot, visceral body mass and mantle, often protected by a shell. Many withdraw into a spiral shell and close off the aperture with a covering called an operculum. During their larval stages, all gastropods go through a body-change process called torsion, or twisting. The mantle cavity moves from the rear position and comes to rest over the head, facing forward toward incoming water. Inside the mantle cavity are the gills, anus, renal and reproductive organs. See pages 74–121.

CLASS BIVALVIA: BIVALVES

Bivalves include mussels, scallops, cockles, oysters, clams and shipworms. These are two-shelled aquatic molluscs, bilaterally symmetrical and laterally compressed. The mantle cavity contains a respiratory chamber and the food-gathering mechanism; it also discharges waste and reproductive products, while the mantle secretes the shell. Most bivalves have a well-developed foot that is used for burrowing or creeping, while others, such as oysters, have lost the use of the foot completely. Most are sedentary and may live either on or in the substrate. See pages 122–127.

Phylum Echinodermata: Echinoderms
CLASS ASTEROIDEA: SEA STARS
Like all echinoderms, sea stars are radially symmetrical, with nearly equal units arranged in a circle, usually based upon multiples of five. They have a unique water vascular system using tubes to carry water throughout the body. Hydraulically driven tube feet do most of the work, including locomotion, adhesion, sensory detection, food capture and respiration. Sea stars are star-shaped or pentagonal. They have a set of calcareous plates embedded into the fleshy tissue of the body wall. The mouth is at the centre of the undersurface. When feeding, the sack-like stomach moves out through the mouth and partly digests food outside the body. See pages 128–131.

CLASS OPHIUROIDEA: BRITTLE STARS
These have a distinct central disc and five slender arms. The arms are solid, not hollow. Brittle stars move with sinuous flexing of arms rather than movement of tube feet. They feed on small organic particles. See page 132.

CLASS ECHINOIDEA: SEA URCHINS
Globular or flattened animals, these have an outer, solid, skeletal structure called a test, which consists of hundreds of interlocking, spine-bearing, calcareous plates. The test is divided into five segments. All wall plates carry movable spines, hinged onto knob-shaped tubercles. The primary spines may vary in shape, while secondary spines usually have little sculpture. Sea urchins are scavengers that feed on algae and animal remains.They move on hydraulic tube feet. See pages 132–134.

CLASS HOLOTHUROIDEA: SEA CUCUMBERS
Slug-like in form, sea cucumbers often crawl with one side of the body in contact with substrate or lie buried in soft sediments. The mouth is at the front end, with the anus at the rear end. They eat plankton and detritus. See page 135.

Phylum Chordata: Protochordates and Vertebrates
CLASS ASCIDIACEA: ASCIDIANS
Although ascidians do not have a vertebral column in adulthood, the larvae show features common to vertebrates. Free-swimming larvae have a notochord (pre-vertebral column), dorsal nerve chord, and pharyngeal clefts or gill slits. These features are lost or changed after settling into the adult stage. See page 136.

CLASS AVES: BIRDS
Australia has 745 species of birds of which 383 are endemic. About 100 species are common to very uncommon seabirds, 15 are resident shorebirds, 30 are common migrant shorebirds, with a further 26 being uncommon migrant shorebirds. Rocky and sandy shores are used by only a few species, such as the Silver Gull and the Crested Tern. See page 137.

External features of seashore organisms

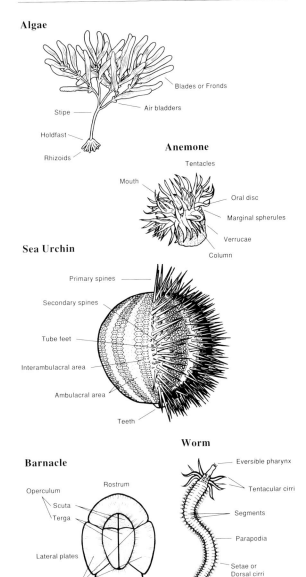

Algae

Blades or Fronds
Air bladders
Stipe
Holdfast
Rhizoids

Anemone

Tentacles
Mouth
Oral disc
Marginal spherules
Verrucae
Column

Sea Urchin

Primary spines
Secondary spines
Tube feet
Interambulacral area
Ambulacral area
Teeth

Worm

Eversible pharynx
Tentacular cirri
Segments
Parapodia
Setae or Dorsal cirri

Barnacle

Rostrum
Operculum
Scuta
Terga
Lateral plates
Marginal plates
Carina

Chiton

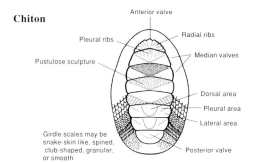

Anterior valve

Radial ribs

Pleural ribs

Median valves

Pustulose sculpture

Dorsal area

Pleural area

Lateral area

Girdle scales may be
snake-skin like, spined,
club-shaped, granular,
or smooth

Posterior valve

Crustacean — Decapod Crab

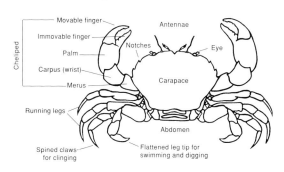

Movable finger

Antennae

Immovable finger

Cheliped

Palm

Notches

Eye

Carpus (wrist)

Merus

Carapace

Running legs

Abdomen

Spined claws
for clinging

Flattened leg tip for
swimming and digging

Mollusc — Univalve Gastropod

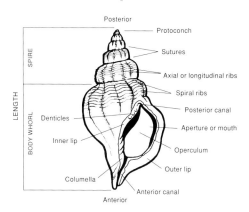

Posterior

Protoconch

SPIRE

Sutures

Axial or longitudinal ribs

Spiral ribs

LENGTH

Posterior canal

Denticles

Aperture or mouth

BODY WHORL

Inner lip

Operculum

Outer lip

Columella

Anterior canal

Anterior

Key to symbols

Algae p. 20–29

Sponge p. 30

Anemones, Corals and Hydroids
p. 31–36

Worm p. 37–39

Barnacle p. 40–44

Slater p. 45

Crab p. 46–68

Chiton p. 69–73

Abalone p. 74

Limpet p. 75–85

Gastropod p. 86–116

Siphon Shell p. 117–119

Sea Hare p. 120–121

Bivalve p. 122–127

Seastar p. 128–132

Urchin p. 133–134

Holothurian p. 135

Cunjevoi p. 136

Gull p. 137

Safety and field hints

Tides and Waves Plan to arrive at the shore about an hour before low tide. Be aware of the time the tide will turn; then you will need to retreat back up the shore. The shipping or weather section of the local newspaper will list daily tides. You can also purchase tide tables from newsagents or fishing goods stores.

The most serious safety issue for rocky shore explorers is the threat to life caused by a freak wave that surges over the rocky shore, ambushing the unwary. An unsuspecting person can easily be washed into a deep gutter or off a rock into deep water, and either drown or be swept against barnacle-encrusted rocks. No matter how safe a rocky shore may appear, never turn your back to the waves, and always keep a lookout for infrequent large waves.

Always move slowly on slippery algae shores. If a large wave is approaching, get a firm foothold, brace yourself side-on to the wave, leaning slightly into it to retain your balance. Never run from a wave. You may fall or be pushed over by the wall of water.

Dangerous Animals: Don't try to catch or pick up the Blue-ringed Octopus, anemone cone shells, sea snakes, box jellyfish, sea jellies or bluebottles. They can all inflict a painful — or even a fatal — sting. If someone has been stung or bitten, immobilise the bitten part with a splint and commence mouth-to-mouth expired air resuscitation if the patient has any difficulty breathing. Get medical help immediately. The patient may lose consciousness, but keep up the resuscitation until help arrives.

Sun Protection: When visiting any ocean shore, remember to 'slip, slop, slap'. Slip on a shirt with a collar, slop 15+ sun-cream on any uncovered skin, and slap on a wide-brimmed hat. Don't wear a cap that leaves your neck unprotected. You will be sunburned in just 15 minutes without proper protection.

Footwear: Wear an old pair of lace up sandshoes with good tread. Wear old socks, to stop your heels from being chafed. Don't wear thongs or sandals.

ROCKY SHORE CONSERVATION CODE

- Tread carefully and avoid stepping on marine animals or algae when walking across a rock platform or seashore. Your weight will kill most animals and dislodge algae.
- Avoid catching rock pool animals. Rough handling may damage their skin or they may dry out if removed from the water. You may learn more by patiently observing animals in their own habitat. Write down your observations before you forget them.
- Many shore animals are found under rocks and boulders. Roll rocks over carefully, in order to look underneath, but remember also to return them carefully to their original position, so as not to damage any creatures found there.
- Do not litter; collect and properly dispose of any litter found.
- Some rocky ocean shores are marine protected areas or aquatic reserves, where all the creatures and algae are protected from any interference by humans. You may visit these shores but their animals and algae should remain unharmed and untouched.
- When you visit a rocky ocean shore, don't remove an animal from its habitat. This gives it no chance of leaving further offspring, to repopulate its environment.

Sea Lettuce *Ulva species* 100–150mm

The common name 'Sea Lettuce' describes this algae's form well: a broad, grass-green, thin, transparent single frond emerging from a small holdfast. The leaf, or thallus, is often entire but may be divided into ruffled branches. Once considered a single cosmopolitan species, Sea Lettuce have now been divided by researchers into a number of species, including six related forms from southern Australian shores. All species of Sea Lettuce occur at low-tide levels and in rock pools on flat platform areas constantly being washed by breaking waves. *Ulva species* grow luxuriantly during winter and seem to prefer waters enriched by organic waste.

Green Bait Weed *Enteromorpha intestinalis* 20–150mm

This algae forms dense, turf-like growths. It is easily identified by its long, medium to dark green, thin, tubular, unbranched fronds and moderately large polygonal (five-sided) cells. The holdfast is formed by root-like extensions called rhizoids, growing from the plant's base. The unbranched, tubular threads are partly filled with gas. Fronds are narrow, transparent ribbons and are hair-like in form. This is a cosmopolitan species that is found in most oceans. It is very common around Australian shores. It occurs at high-tide levels and above, in damp regions where fresh water soaks out from a cliff.

Bubble Weed *Chaetomorpha coliformis* 100–400mm

This algae is distinguished by its light to deep green, densely clustered, unbranched, long fronds, made up of chains of large, rounded cells. It is usually attached to another plant. When living, the cells are rounded but they collapse when dried out. This species ranges from Walkerville in Victoria to Venus Bay, Eyre

Peninsula in SA and probably around Tasmania. It occurs at the low-tide fringe and below to 4m, on rock and attached to other algae. It is found on moderate to rough-water coasts, or in rock pools. It was formerly known as *C. darwinii*.

Green Sea Velvet *Codium fragile* 50–300mm

The Green Sea Velvet is an erect, much-branched, black-green to bottle-green algae. It has rounded, finely branched, cylindrical fronds that are packed close together. These fronds grow to 300mm, are 6mm thick and are often split into two equal parts. When observed under water, fine hairs can be seen all over the branches. The basal disc is broad, spongy and soft. This species ranges from Ballina, NSW, around the south-eastern shores to Victor Harbor, SA, and also Tasmania. It inhabits cooler temperate waters of both hemispheres and occurs at the lowest tide levels and below, as well as intertidal pools on rocky coasts subjected to high-energy waves.

21

Halimeda *Halimeda cuneata* 150mm

This bright green algae is distinguished by its unusual shape and segmentation. It has branches of wide, flattened, hard segments strengthened by calcium, joined by more flexible segments. It attaches itself to rock by its holdfast, which consists of numerous fine threads. This species ranges from Recherche Archipelago in WA, to Caloundra in southern Queensland and is also found in southern Africa. It is typically found on rocky shores in gutters and on coral reefs at low-tide level and below to 7m.

Caulerpa *Caulerpa filiformis* 200mm

Caulerpa is a seaweed with a dense mass of bright green, small strap-like leaves called ramuli, each measuring 100–200mm long and 5mm wide. The carti-lage-like stem of the plant, called a stolon, grows flat along the rock attached by fine out-growths. Arising from the stolon are five rows of photosynthetic ram-uli, each of which tapers

to a short, blunt, spinous tip. In Australia, this species occurs only in NSW but recent research reveals that it also occurs in South Africa. It is found at low-tide levels along the edges of rock platforms and in gutters, on medium- to high-energy coasts, down to 40m. It can be found near Cunjevoi at low-tide level.

Ectocarpus *Ectocarpus siliculosus* 10–250mm

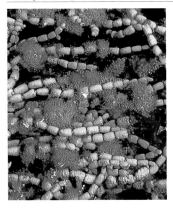

This light brown to buff-coloured, hair-like algae is found in pools at high-tide levels. It is often seen as a fine hairy growth on other algae, particularly on **Neptune's Necklace** (see page 26). This species has no basal disc, nor does it have a stem. It is diffuse and unstructured in shape, with a lot of irregular branching from the attachment point, which gradually tapers into intertangled, long, fine hairs. Widely distributed in temperate and

tropical seas, this common species ranges from southern Queensland all around the southern shores, including Tasmania, to at least Rottnest Island in WA.

Sausage Weed *Splachnidium rugosum* 80–200mm

This distinctive medium to dark brown algae has short, swollen stems filled with a gelatinous material that makes it look like a clump of small, wrinkled sausages. This plant has a small, disc-shaped hold-fast. Sausage Weed ranges from Newcastle, NSW, around the southern shores to Point Sinclair in SA and is also found in South Africa, New Zealand and some northerly sub-Antarctic islands. It forms

a distinctive band at the mid-tide level on coasts exposed to moderate to rough water. When exposed at low tide, it hangs down across the rock face.

Doubling Weed *Dictyota dichotoma* 150–200mm

This algae characteristically has fronds that regularly branch into equal parts and these maintain the same width along their entire length. The fronds are flat, about 1cm wide and up to 20cm long. The holdfast is made up of single-strand outgrowths called rhizoids. The reproductive cells are either scattered or form patterns over the frond surface.

While this species is mostly medium brown, slightly darker near the base, it often appears bluish when seen under water. It ranges from southern Queensland around the southern shores to south-eastern WA. Widespread in temperate waters, it extends into subtropical and colder waters. This species occurs at the lowest tide levels and below.

Padina *Padina pavonea* 40–120mm

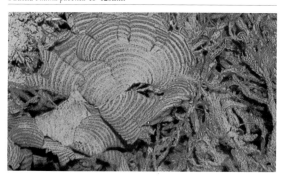

This distinctive, common algae has thin, fan-shaped fronds with concentric markings and rolled edges that become dissected with age. The plant attaches to the rock by thread-like outgrowths called rhizoids. Light olive-brown in colour, it has lighter concentric markings.

Padina is a tropical genus that has 2–3 species extending down through NSW and WA into southern waters. *Padina pavonea* ranges along eastern Australia. Found at the low-tide fringe and below on rocky ocean shores, it usually occurs in rock pools and reef fringes in moderately exposed situations. It exposes its open fronds to light but not to dry air.

Globe Algae *Colpomenia sinuosa* 40–60mm

Irregular in shape, this globular, crinkled algae is sometimes twice as high as it is broad. Its skin membrane is a thin, crisp wall filled with water and air. The plant is usually attached to other algae, seagrasses or rock by a small, crusty base. Light yellow or honey-brown to dark brown, it is widely

found in most oceans, including all those around Australia. Globe Algae prefers tropical and temperate shores and is common in summer. It occurs at mid-tide level and below and is usually found in rock pools and in estuaries. It is the most common species of globe-shaped algae found attached to other plants in southern Australia.

Bull Kelp *Durvillaea potatorum* 7m

This is a most impressive, medium to dark brown kelp with long, thick, leathery, strap-like fronds that may grow up to 7m long and 30cm wide. Its disc-shaped holdfast (shown in photograph) is 5–25cm across and up to 4cm thick. Bull Kelp ranges from Bermagui, NSW, around the south-eastern shores to Cape Jaffa in SA. It prefers coasts that are subjected to rough water. At low tide, the massive fan-shaped fronds can be seen swirling back and forth in the surge. It is found just below low-tide level down to 10m. This kelp is harvested commercially for sodium alginate, which is used as a gel in toothpaste and icecream.

Leather Kelp *Eklonia radiata*

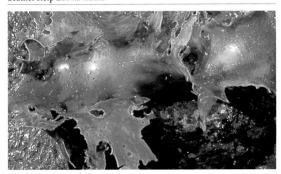

This is the most common large kelp seen along southern Australian coasts. From the conical holdfast, a long rounded stem (0.3–2m) ends with a broad, flat, strap-like blade. From this central blade, side fronds (5–20cm long, 1–10cm wide) occur on both sides. These fronds have a rough, crinkled surface armed with short spines (2–4mm long). Colour is medium to dark brown. Leather Kelp ranges from Caloundra in southern Queensland, around the southern shores to Houtman Abrolhos in WA. This species occurs from the lowest tide level to below on coasts affected by moderate to rough wave action. It is often found washed ashore after severe storms.

Neptune's Necklace *Hormosira banksii* 100–300mm

Sometimes called 'sea grapes', this distinctive dark brown algae is made up of strings of water-filled, oval-shaped beads joined together by a short stalk. The fronds may be 100–300mm long, with each bead 15mm in diameter. The outside sur-

face of each bead is roughened by pores that contain the reproductive cells. Neptune's Necklace ranges from Port Macquarie in NSW, around the southern shores to King George Sound in WA. It often forms vast colonies covering most of the rock surface at mid-tide levels down to low-tide levels on rocky shores.

Strap Weed *Phyllospora comosa* 0.5–2m

This strap weed, with its distinctive light olive-green fronds with a yellow to golden tint, swashes around in surging water. It has saw-tooth-edged fronds and many spindle-shaped float bladders at the ends of its short stalks, but not at the base of its leafy fronds. The air-filled bladders keep the fronds upright so they are more exposed to sunlight. This species ranges from Port Macquarie in NSW, around the south-eastern shores to Robe in SA. It is common on rough-water coasts at the lowest tide levels and below to 18m and in deep pools.

Brown Seaweed *Cystophora torulosa* 1.5m

This seaweed has a flattened zig-zag shape, with club-shaped fertile branchlets (receptacles) clustered along it. These receptacles are long (20–70mm) and 2–4mm wide. The overall colour is yellow-brown to dark brown. Its mainland distribution is limited—from Wilsons Promontory to Apollo Bay in Victoria—but it is found all around Tasmania and the Bass Strait islands, as well as in New Zealand. It occurs at the lowest tide levels and below on sheltered reefs. This species is often found just below the band of **Neptune's Necklace** (see page 26). *Cystophora torulosa* is a dominant algae at the lowest tide levels.

Geniculate Coralline Algae *Amphiroa anceps* 200mm

The branched, rigid, segmented stems of this coralline algae are hardened with lime (calcium carbonate). The segments are connected at slender flexible nodes known as geniculae. This algae has an important ecological role, especially in the tropics, as the calcium carbonate cements dead coral skeletal remains together into a solid structure. Pinkish when alive, it becomes white when bleached by the sun. It ranges all around the Australian mainland and northern Tasmania. Western specimens have wider stems than those occurring in the east. It occurs on moderately exposed reef and horizontal platforms, from low-tide level down to 12m. This is the most common branched coralline algae found on the eastern and south-west coasts of Australia.

Iridescent Algae *Champia compressa* 25mm

This very small red algae has tiny, flattened, ragged fronds. It does not appear red at all—as water swirls in a rock-pool or a gutter, a sudden flash of its brilliant blue-green iridescence can catch the eye. When removed from the water,

this colour disappears. It is not a real pigment but is caused by the diffraction of light. The true colour is a translucent brown or red. Under a microscope, each frond appears hollow, swollen and oval. Each little frond bears one or two side branches. This species is found at extreme low-tide levels and in pools on rocky ocean shores.

Encrusting Corallines *Corallinaceae* species

The stony, calcified, pink crusts of many coralline algae species form flat expanses over rocks, or on other plants and mollusc shells. While extremely common, most kinds cannot be properly identified without knowing their internal structure. They prefer to grow in shaded locations and often form a nearly continuous cover over the floor and wall of tidal pools, as well as in moist areas of rock platforms. Some species can grow up to 10mm in thickness. The reproductive structures of the corallines are often inconspicuous. In the tropics, encrusting coralline algae help to build the reefs.

Coralline Seaweed *Corallina officinalis* 25mm

A feather-like red algae with very small, fine, neatly jointed branches. Thickened main stems, made up of jointed segments, extend in straight rows from the hold-fast. Along each stem, at every second or third joint, on each side lateral, jointed branches grow. From each branched joint, other spikes emerge to form a flattened,

feather-like frond. Widespread in its distribution all around Australia, it occurs commonly in rock pools and on moist rock surfaces at the low-tide level. These plants are very conspicuous when they have been dried out by the sun and form distinctive limy white tufts on the rocks. '*Officinalis*' means this algae was formerly used as a medicine, once regularly kept in a pharmacist's stock to be used as an antacid.

29

Sponges *Porifera*

 Sponges are simple animals that live permanently attached to the ocean floor and lack distinct tissues and organs. They have no nervous system or power of locomotion. The basic functions of life, such as feeding, oxygen uptake and waste removal, are carried out by specialised individual cells. Sponges have a single layer of outer cells, an internal layer of cells within feeding chambers and an internal matrix of organic and mineral supporting structures. The skeletal material is made up of spongin, a fibrous protein, and crystalline needle-like spicules of various shapes, depending upon the species. Sponges are filter-feeders. Their bodies are organised around a system of water canals. Water is drawn in through pores. Cells called choanocytes each have a single flagellum. These flagella beat in unison to produce a flow of water through the sponge. Incoming food sticks to cell walls and becomes trapped. Most of the food sponges process is so small it cannot be seen under an ordinary microscope. Sponges pass their own volume of water in ten seconds. Identification of sponges is difficult: researchers must

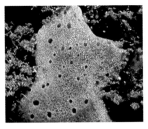 rely on the size and shape of the spicules because colour is no indication and sponge shape varies with the environment. The same species may be flat and encrusting, or tall and bulky, depending on whether it is subjected to heavy wave action or found in sheltered waters. Sponges grow best in areas of strong water current.

Waratah Anemone *Actinia tenebrosa* 40mm

This vivid anemone is commonly seen in its contracted globular state, looking like a blob of brownish jelly with a hole in the middle. Seeing it under water is a different story. Here it has a rich-red, smooth and squat column, a light red oral disc, very light red tentacles and iridescent blue bumps on the column that contain stinging nematocysts.

The tentacles are short, numerous and tapering. This species ranges from NSW around the southern shores to southern WA and is also found in New Zealand. It occurs at mid- to low-tide levels in crevices and on undersurfaces of rocks on semi-protected and exposed rocky shores. It clones its young inside its column.

Anemone *Phlyctenanthus australis* 100mm

This large anemone has a large column and is similar to the orange-coloured, free-moving *Phlyctenactis tuberculosa*, except that this species remains permanently attached to the reef. *Phlyctenanthus australis* has bulbous, close-set, blue-grey swellings called vesicles on the bluish-white to grey-green column and has up to 100 short, conical, reddish-brown tentacles with blunt tips. It ranges from Sydney, around the southern shores to the Great Australian Bight, SA, and including Tasmania. It occurs on rocky shores and reefs, at the low-tide fringe and below to 15m depth, on moderate- to high-energy shores.

Eastern Sand Anemone *Oulactis muscosa* 60–80mm

This large anemone is found in sand-filled cracks, with sand and bits of shell among its tentacles. Usually only the oral disc and tentacles are visible. The column is greenish-grey to off-white, with rows of darker bumps called verrucae. The oral disc may be red, green, black or white, with darker streaks radiating from the mouth. Three rows of short tentacles, pale greenish to greyish-white, are marked with horizontal black bands. This species ranges from southern Queensland around the southern shores to east of Spencer Gulf, SA, and also New Zealand. It occurs on sand-covered rocky areas, usually in water-filled crevices.

Southern Sand Anemone *Oulactis macmurrichi* 60–80mm

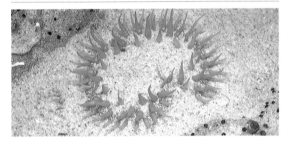

This anemone differs from the Sand Anemone (above) because the column is reddish-brown or green to light purple in colour, with light green tentacles. It ranges from Coffin Bay, South Australia, around the south-western shores to Perth, WA. This species is found on rocky shores subjected to low-ranging to high-energy waves, at mid- to low-tidal levels and in rock pools. Both anemones occur in similar habitats and exhibit the same behaviour. Except for the slight difference in coloration, there is little to distinguish them. Indeed, they may not actually be separate species.

Green Anemone *Cnidopus verater* 50–70mm

This anemone is a uniform emerald- to olive-green, occasionally brown, with lighter green tentacles. The column has a prominent row of bumps at the base, which decrease in size toward the top, where it is smooth. Like **Sand Anemone** (see opposite page), sand grains and bits of shell are often attached to the column. The smooth, narrow tentacles are 4cm long and without markings. This species ranges from southern Queensland around southern shores to southern WA, including Tasmania. The Green Anemone occurs in rock pools and crevices on rocky coasts with moderate wave energy.

Tropical Sand Anemone *Heteractis malu* 100mm

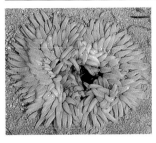
This is a quite distinctive, wide-bodied, squat sand anemone. It has hundreds of small, very light brown to whitish tentacles arranged in rows around the oral disc. A large tropical species, it extends down the West Australian coast as far as Perth. It is widespread in the Indo–West Pacific region. It occurs at the low-tide fringe and below to

18m depth, in sand and shell-rubble habitats, along the edge of seagrass beds.

Zoanthid *Protopalythoa australiensis* 5–7mm

Protopalythoa species are anemone-like animals called zoanthids that are joined together at the base of separate polyps. These polyps do not secrete a skeleton as do corals, but incorporate sediments into their bodies during growth, which support the tiny animals inside. The tentacles are often short and the colour of the oral disc is usually dark brown or dark green. These species range across tropical Australia and occur on shallow reefs and rocky shores, sometimes exposed at the lowest tides. Formerly called *Gemmaria* species. The lack of a skeleton makes identification among the various species quite difficult.

By-the-wind Sailer *Velella velella* 10–15mm

This blue organism consists of a floating disc about 15mm across, with a thin S-shaped sail across the top. Although there are no tentacles, it does contain bands of stinging cells called nematocysts, which are used to trap food as the organism is driven by the wind across the water surface. The floating disc consists of a set of air chambers, which keep the colony afloat and upright. There are right-handed and left-handed forms, which ensures that they are not all blown ashore together. Although not an intertidal dweller, it is an occasional visitor, brought in by ocean currents from the tropical north. It then gets blown ashore by north-easterly winds.

Blue Coral *Heliopora coerulea* to 3m

The Blue Coral gets its name from the indigo-blue colour of a freshly broken surface. It is normally greyish-blue to greyish-green with white polyps. This is not a true scleratinian coral and its family Helioporidae is represented by only a single genus and a single species. It has a wide range of forms, which are usually dependent on the environmental conditions. It may be plant-like, plate-like or columnar. It ranges from North West Cape, WA, to Bowen, Queensland. It is a

common coral, sometimes dominant, found on tropical reef flats and the upper reef slopes as well as on some shores.

Double-faced Coral *Turbinaria bifrons* 1000mm

Colonies of this coral start as a flat laminate, and later grow into long, upright, double-faced fronds. The small coral animals are all similar, cone-shaped and regularly spaced. The tentacles are grey, brown or green with a darker wart-like part of the polyp wall into which the tentacled part of the polyp retracts. Colonies may be very large and are either plate-like or foliage-like. These colonies often vary in form, depending on whether they are found in shallow or deeper waters, due to the effects of available light. Unlike most corals, all species of *Turbinaria* breed in autumn when sea temperatures fall. They are common along eastern Australian tropical shores but uncommon on the west coast. They extend into the tidal zone when attached to a rocky substrate.

35

Glomerate Soft Coral *Dendronephthya klunzingeri* 1000mm

Colonies of this soft coral are plant-like in form. The sparsely branched, equal-length stalks diverge from one another, ending in bundles of polyps crowded together into cauliflower-like bunches. The common name 'glomerate' means compactly clustered. When fully expanded at night, this coral may reach a height of more than 1m. When contracted, the polyps appear as clusters, protected by protruding hardened spines called spicules. This soft coral is brightly coloured, often red, orange or yellow. It ranges across tropical northern Australia. On some shores, it may be exposed at low tide, so that the fronds sag and look quite floppy. This species may occur in areas where the water is turbid.

Coral *Goniophora lobata* 200–1000mm

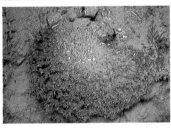

Goniophora corals either form columns or broad, massive colonies. They may also form thin crusts across rock surfaces. Its usual form is a rounded, lobed colony about 200mm across. The coral hard parts, called corallites, have thick but porous walls. The

polyps have 24 long, fleshy tentacles. Because it extends these by day as well as night, this species is easily mistaken for a soft coral. An aggressive species, it may attack any other coral within reach. It is usually grey, brown or green in colour. It ranges across tropical Australia and occurs on reef flats, lagoons and slopes but is also commonly found in turbid, muddy waters on shores protected from strong wave action.

Eunice *Eunice aphroditois* 500–1000mm

Eunice is a long, multi-segmented, robust-bodied predatory worm and one of the largest polychaetes in the world. It has two eyes and five tentacles. Its unusual feeding structure, called a pharynx, turns inside out to capture prey. Sharp mandibles at the pharynx end can give a nasty bite. There are numerous body segments and on the sides of each ring is a pair of movement lobes called parapodia, tipped with bundles of bristle-setae. Overall colour is dark purple-brown to red-brown, with a purple iridescence. There is a white ring around the fourth body segment. Widespread around the world, in Australia this species ranges around the southern shores. It occurs under stones lying in sand or mud at low-tide level, and below, on rocky shores.

Bristle Worm or Fire Worm *Eurythoe complanata* 120–140mm

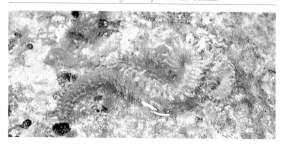

The Bristle Worm is distinguished by its long, stout body with few segments, its salmon-pink colour and the numerous setae around its body that form a snow-white fringe. Like **Eunice** (see above), it shoots out its mouthparts to catch prey. Its movement limbs, called parapodia, have two stems each. Gills are arranged in branching tufts. The setae fringes are made of extremely brittle calcium carbonate spikes, which can stick into fingers and break off, causing a sting. The setae are hollow and contain venom, which can cause great irritation. This species has a world-wide range and is widespread around Australia. It is common under rocks on coastal platforms or dead coral on sandy reef flats.

Galeolaria *Galeolaria caespitosa* 20–30mm

While *Galeolaria* worms may exist singly, they are more commonly found in colonies. A colony may be so thick and dense that it forms a distinctive microhabitat for many other creatures. The worm builds white to grey calcareous tubes up to 30mm long. Its head crown holds a stalked and spine-winged tube cover, called an operculum, and tentacles, which are used as gills for gas exchange and to capture food. *Galeolaria* ranges from southern Queensland around the southern shores to WA. Scattered tubes may be found anywhere on a shore, even above the highest tides, moistened only by spray.

Idanthyrsus *Idanthyrsus pennatus* 50mm

Idanthyrsus is tube-dwelling worm of the family *Sabellidae* that lives singly or in dense colonies. The tubes are composed of cemented sand grains and shell particles. They are irregular in form and very hard in consistency. The worm inside the tube has a body that is divided into four segments. This species ranges from south-eastern Queensland all around southern Australia. Along the southern and south-eastern shores, *Idanthyrsus* is found in single tubes constructed under stones at and below the low-water mark on rocky shores. North of Coffs Harbour in NSW, it tends to form communities that consist of cemented-together masses of tubes. Sabellid worms are filter feeders.

Scale Worm *Lepidonotus melanogrammus* 30–50mm

The Scale Worm is a short, compact worm with 12 pairs of overlapping scales, called elytra, covering the upper surface. Each scale is marked with a distinctive C-shaped brown pattern. If touched, the scales may be shed. This worm has two pairs of eyes and two single side antennae. It is light fawn to grey in colour. The Scale Worm occurs in NSW, SA and southern WA. It is found at low-tide levels on rocky shores, usually under stones. This active predator captures its food with an eversible armed pharynx, which swiftly inverts like the finger on a rubber glove. The sharp mandibles at the end are used for capturing unsuspecting prey.

Peanut Worm *Phascolosoma noduliferum* 12–65mm

The Peanut Worm has a flask-shaped, almost cylindrical body, which is pointed at the front end. When resting, its body is normally introverted, like a finger of a glove turned in on itself, but when seeking prey, the animal can extend itself rapidly. The mouth, mandibles and feeding tentacles are at the front end of this extrovert. The Peanut Worm's body lacks segmentation but is covered with fine granules. Colour is brown to light brown, slightly darker at the ends. It is very similar to its relation *P. annulatum*. The Peanut Worm ranges from Port Stephens in NSW, around the southern shores to Hopetoun in WA, and around Tasmania. It occurs on sheltered and moderately exposed reefs at low-tide levels and below to 1500m. It is usually found under stones embedded in sand or gravel, or in *Galeolaria* tube-worm colonies (see page 38).

Surf Barnacle *Catomerus polymerus* 25–30mm

The Surf Barnacle is distinctively flattened with eight main plates surrounded by many smaller plates that become smaller toward the base. Even when eroded, the outer plates are still distinctive. The exterior is grey-white with a greenish tinge. This species ranges from mid-NSW around the southern shores to southern WA. It occurs on most rocky ocean shores exposed to high-energy waves. The common name shows its preference for heavy wave action and spray. It is found in large numbers on some vertical rock faces, usually just above the tube-worm *Galeolaria* zone (see page 38). It may form a zone if in large numbers.

Six-plated Barnacle *Chthamalus antennatus* 16–18mm

The Six-plated Barnacle is medium size with six non-porous main shell plates. The sutures between the plates are easily seen. The middle opercular valve margins create an irregular-shaped cross. The exterior is dirty white to grey and, on some, the shell tips have eroded to form a small, white, shiny area that looks like tooth enamel. This species ranges from NSW to north-eastern Tasmania. It occurs at high levels on the shore, often above mean high-tide level. Because it lives so high up, it may be covered by water only a few times each month to feed. It is often found with the **Honeycomb Barnacle** (see page 42), which is smaller and has only four main plates.

Malayan Barnacle *Chthamalus malayensis* 8–17mm

This variable, six-plated, tropical barnacle grows on mangroves, molluscs and other barnacles, with a different form for each. It is taller, more conical and more distinctly ribbed than its other tropical relatives, with 4–6 ribs per plate and these ribs may split into two toward the shell edge. Generally ash-grey in colour, it ranges from Shark Bay in WA, north across to Hervey Bay in Queensland. It favours areas with increased wave action and more stable saltiness, such as on rocky reefs or near open water where it is not too muddy. It can occupy a wide band of rock face, sometimes at quite high levels. Some may be exposed 90 per cent of the time at 35°C.

Wither's Barnacle *Chthamalus withersii* 8–16mm

This flattened, six-plated, tropical barnacle has a sub-circular shape and wavy outline, without distinct ribs and has simple non-interlocking suture lines. The large orifice is diamond-shaped and inside the feeding plate the suture lines are straight. It is a

drably coloured greenish-grey, or ash-grey where eroded. This species ranges across the tropics from the northern Kimberley in WA to Hervey Bay in southern Queensland. It occurs between high- to mid-tide levels on intertidal rocks, wharf piles and mangroves, where it prefers crevices or shady areas. It is tolerant of considerable fluctuations of salinity and muddiness in seawater, so it is also found at river mouths and in mangrove swamps. It is normally found higher on ocean rocky shores than **Malayan Barnacle** (see above).

41

Honeycomb Barnacle *Chamaesipho tasmanica* 5–8mm

This small barnacle has four main non-porous shell plates. Colonies occur crowded together in such vast numbers that it is difficult to distinguish separate plates. The opercular valve edges (on top) form a regular cross. If uneroded, these barnacles are mostly grey to white, while eroded specimens are brownish. This species ranges from NSW to Tasmania, and also New Zealand. By far the most numerous barnacle, this species occurs on exposed rock surfaces on open coast at mid- to high-tide levels. It is found only on rocks (never on wood) and may cover such large areas of rock surface that nothing but barnacles are visible. Previously this species was known as *Chamaesipho columna*.

Rose-coloured Barnacle *Tesseropora rosea* 20mm

Young specimens of this tall, conical barnacle are grey to white in colour. Older barnacles may be more eroded, showing more pink colour. There are four main wall plates, with a five-sided orifice on top. Inside the plates is porous, broken by radial walls. This species ranges from NSW to north-eastern Victoria and is occasionally found in north-eastern Tasmania. It occurs at mid- to high-tide levels on exposed coasts where wave action is

moderate to strong, often fully exposed to raging surf. Like all barnacles, the Rose-coloured Barnacle feeds on plankton using its basket-like feeding arms called cirri.

Rosette Barnacle *Tetraclitella purpurascens* 20–25mm

This barnacle has a distinctive, rough, scaly appearance. It has a very low, wide shell made up of four shell plates and in uneroded barnacles, where these shell plates are distinct, the orifice is diamond-shaped. Inside the the plates is finely porous, forming a honeycomb pattern. The exterior is grey-white, with a mauve or greenish tinge. The Rosette Barnacle ranges from Queensland around the southern shores to WA. It occurs at all levels on rocky ocean shores up

to high-water levels. It is always found in protected and semi-protected areas where it prefers crevices or shelters under boulders in the shade. It is sensitive to being dried out by the sun.

Scaly Barnacle *Tetraclitella squamosa* 25–30mm

The tropical Scaly Barnacle is taller, larger, and more conical than the temperate **Rosette Barnacle** (see above), which has a similar scale pattern. Its rough exterior is made up of a large number of flattened scales of similar size. There are four distinct shell plates, with the relationship between the shell plates clear. The orifice is diamond-shaped and the colour is grey to brown, often stained with mud from the habitat. This species has an Indo-Pacific distribution and in

Australia it ranges from northern WA, across the northern shores and down the coast of central Queensland. It occurs high on rocky shores, often on vertical rock faces and frequently in large groups.

Giant Rock Barnacle *Balanus nigrescens* 30–60mm

A very large barnacle, this species has a distinctive blue mantle inside the operculum. The six distinct steep-sided marginal plates are marked with transverse lines. Colour is normally white to pale green but the shell plates are often eroded and encrusted with marine algae and organisms. This species ranges from NSW, across the southern shores to WA and, while rare in Tasmania, it is common on some Bass Strait islands. Found low on the shore at and below low-tide level on rocky shores, it prefers a steep rock face that is pounded by medium to strong waves. It occurs singly or in groups.

Barnacle *Balanus trigonus* 18–20mm

This relatively small, steeply conical barnacle has six shell plates and is deep pink in colour, with roughened white ribs. The orifice is triangular, with characteristic rows of pits on the top plates. This species is recorded in all Australian States, although it is normally found only in the protected waters of

estuaries with oysters and mussels, and on kelp holdfasts. An important fouling species, it attaches to the hulls of ships and to wharf pilings. On the open coast, this barnacle has an unusual relationship with the **Sowrie Crab** (see page 58). It may lodge on the crab's carapace and legs. It is not known what happens to the barnacle when the crab sheds its carapace.

Blunt-tailed Sea Centipede *Paridotea munda* 22mm

This long, thin crustacean looks like a cross between a prawn and a centipede. Its abdomen is a single segment, with faint sutures and the abdomen end is blunt with two faint bumps at the edges. A close relative, *Paridotea ungulata*, can be distinguished by its sharp tail tips. Usually olive-coloured or pinkish-brown, it occurs on algae the same colour as itself. The specimen photographed was a rich light green, matching the frond of the **Sea Lettuce** it was on (see page 20). The Blunt-tailed Sea Centipede ranges from NSW to South Australia, including Tasmania, and occurs at the low-tide fringe, in pools and gutters down to 3m. It swims using its pleopods.

Marine Slater *Ligia australiensis* 10–15mm

The Marine Slater, a swift, long-legged relative of the Garden Slater, is often seen foraging in the open, high on the ocean shores. Its flattened, oval-shaped body is twice as long as it is wide. This species has a large head with two large eyes and very long antennae, which are longer than the body. The tail telson has three spikes. Colour is slate-grey with lighter and darker patches. The Marine Slater ranges from NSW, south across the southern shores to southern WA. While it seems uncommon on the open coast in NSW it is extremely common in estuaries. Along the southern shores it can be highly abundant, hiding under all forms of shelter.

45

Terrestrial Hermit Crab *Coenoloita variabilis* 40mm

This small hermit crab is found on sandy shores behind mangroves, hiding under debris and rocks. It lives in spiral mollusc shells, regularly swapping shells as soon as it finds a more suitable one. The hermit crab has large gill chambers that can hold water. As long as the gill filaments are kept moist, the crab is able to wander far from water. The Terrestrial Hermit Crab has fewer spines on its carapace and legs than other hermit crabs. Cream to pale brown in colour, it also has darker markings. This species ranges from Exmouth Gulf in WA, across the northern shores to north Queensland. It occurs inter-tidally and higher, often hundreds of metres above high-tide level.

Half Crab *Petrolisthes elongatus* 8–10mm

Although crab-like, the Half Crab differs from true crabs by having a small last pair of walking legs, a small tail fan, the abdomen folded under the carapace, and very large flattened chelae. It has a smooth carapace with no spines and its antennae are very long but not very hairy. The males are larger than the females and both are green-brown with brownish chelae. Abundant in sheltered bays and reefs around Tasmania, this species is also found in Victoria and New Zealand. A filter feeder, it occurs under rocks near low-tide level and below to 12m, on medium- to high-energy coasts. The family to which this species belongs is more diverse in the tropics.

Hairy Stone Crab *Lomis hirta* 15–25mm

The Hairy Stone Crab is not a true crab. Its last pair of legs are small and hidden under the rear of the carapace, which is flattened and covered with brown, hairy bristles and bead-like granules. It has large, flattened chelipeds and the clawed legs are large and of similar size. Both sexes are similar. It is brown on top with a bluish-white undersurface while its long, hairy antennae and some mouthparts are a vivid blue. This species ranges from central Victoria across southern shores to Bunbury in southern WA, including Tasmania. It occurs at low-tide levels on medium- to high-energy shores, usually under boulders. It feeds by filtering plankton.

Smooth Pebble Crab *Philyra laevis* 20–25mm

This cream or slatey grey coloured crab is almost globe-shaped, with four white dots on the smooth carapace. It has long, spindly chelae and swollen hands; its walking legs are long and slender. This species ranges from Victoria and Tasmania to Albany in WA. It prefers seagrass areas in muddy or sandy bays. At Westernport Bay, as the tide comes in over the large expanse of sandflats, the water's edge moves in at a slow walking pace. The crab can be seen trundling along behind this edge, pushing its hands down into the soft mud and under pebbles, searching for titbits. It is also known as *Dittosa laevis*.

47

Three-pronged Spider Crab *Halicarcinus ovatus* 15–20mm

The spindly walking legs of this small, distinctively shaped crab give it a spider-like appearance. Its legs can make it difficult to disentangle from algae. This species has an unusual beak-like extension of the carapace, called a rostrum, between the eyes. There are no eye notches and the carapace is crossed by fine grooves. The claws of male crabs are larger than those of females. The bold, symmetrical colour pattern includes red-white, red-black and brown-white. This species ranges from Port Stephens in NSW, around all the southern shores to WA. It occurs at low-tide levels among seaweed or under rocks, on rocky shores. It is also abundant in seagrass beds of estuaries.

Seaweed Decorator Crab *Naxia tumida* 30–40mm

This crab's pear-shaped carapace is covered with spines, knobs and fine hooked hairs, in which the crab threads algae, sponges and hydroids to form an effective camouflage. It has a pair of short horns between the eyes. The carapace is yellow-brown, brown or brown-green, but is obscured by all its adornments. The camouflage is so effective that unless the crab is moving, it is rarely detected. This species ranges from central NSW, around the southern shores to Houtman Abrolhos in WA. It occurs at low-tide levels and below, often in rock pools, under rocks or among algae.

Thalamita Crab *Thalamita crenata* 100mm

This highly aggressive, oval-shaped crab is the most common crab on the tropical reef flat. Wide at the front, it tapers to the rear, with the last pair of legs flattened and paddle-like for swimming. The flattened carapace is wider than it is long, with about five sharp spines along the sides. The large, spined chelae have strong claws, ready for self-defence. The carapace is usually greenish-with brown mottling. The tips of the legs and chelae fingers are brown, while the chelae are blue to white. This species ranges across tropical northern Australia. It occurs in intertidal waters and below, often on coral-rubble beaches and on hard mud shores.

Tubercled Crab *Nectocarcinus tuberculosus* 60–70mm

A striking medium-sized crab, this species has a covering of distinctively coloured tubercles on the carapace, legs and chelae, giving it a roughened appearance. It has a brown to reddish-brown base colour and the tubercles are commonly mauve, purple, orange, brown, buff and red. The chelae fingers are black and males have large chelae. The front of the carapace has a distinct notch. This species ranges from Port Jackson in NSW, around the southern shores to Albany, WA. It is found under rocks at the lowest tide levels and below on medium- to low-energy coasts.

Blue-swimmer Crab *Portunus pelagicus* 300mm

The Blue Swimmer is one of the best known edible crabs in Australia. Its carapace is twice as wide as long and it is covered with large granules. In adult males, the large chelipeds are 2–3 times as long as the carapace. The upper colour is mainly blue with paler mottlings, below it is white. The female is smaller and more brownish. Not shore crabs, the Blue Swimmer occurs all around the Australian coastline in sheltered bays and inlets. This species ranges from East Africa, through the Indian and Pacific Oceans to Japan, Tahiti and the north island of New Zealand. They are active, powerful carnivores, only entering shallow water for prey. They are commercially fished in SA and southern Queensland.

Two-spined Burrowing Sand Crab *Matuta planipes* 50mm

This beautifully patterned surf crab is distinguished by its round shape, a pair of side spines and its hind legs, which have become flattened into paddles. The base colour matches its habitat and ranges from white to yellow, with the design varying from dark purple through dark red to brown. This species ranges from mid WA, across the northern shores down to NSW. It occurs on sandy beaches from low-tide down to 7m. Although an excellent swimmer, it prefers to use its rear legs as paddles to burrow quickly backwards into the sand. Unlike other crabs, *Matuta* takes in oxygen-carrying water near its eye sockets and not at the base of the chelipeds.

50

Brown Shawl Crab *Atergatis integerrimus* 120mm

A oval-shaped crab, with an arc-shaped front edge to the carapace. Two-thirds of the way around the carapace edge, a blunt bump divides the front from the sides. The upper surface is convex and quite smooth, without any major spines. The large equal-sized chelae have brown fingers. Colour is uniform light brown to reddish-brown, with a white 'lace-work' mottling on the carapace and brown spotted limbs. A tropical species, the Brown Shawl Crab ranges from Shark Bay in WA, to mid-coastal NSW. It is found intertidally and below to 50m, on rocky, coral or mud shores. This is a dark-fingered crab of the *Xanthidae* family.

Reef Crab *Ozius truncatus* 50–80mm

A gentle crab, its broadly oval-shaped carapace is covered with sparse hairs, granules and distinct knobs. Small but distinct tubercles occur on the front edge and sides of the carapace. The chelae are uneven in size, especially in old males, where the largest chelae is as long as the carapace is wide. Colour varies from dull white in juveniles to rusty brown with olive shades and dark brown mottling in adults. The chelae end is distinctively marked dark brown to black, with lighter coloured finger tips. This species ranges from southern Queensland, around the southern shores to southern WA. It is found at low-tide and below on rocky ocean shores, under rocks and boulders. When disturbed, instead of defending itself, it pretends to be dead.

Bearded Crab *Heteropilumnus fimbriatus* 20–25mm

This small, cream- to buff-coloured crab has a fringe of long silky hairs along the edge of its carapace, which gives it the appearance of a human face with long blond eyebrows — *fimbriatus* means fringed. The upper part of the chelipeds and the edges of the walking legs are also fringed with long hair. This crab has extremely short eye stalks. It has been observed at St. Vincent Gulf in SA and Point Leo at Westernport Bay in Victoria. It is probably found in estuaries across southern Australia. It occurs at low shore levels in a rocky habitat surrounded by sandy mud, and is found sheltering under stones.

Smooth-handed Crab *Pilumnopeus serratifrons* 25–30mm

This is a small, purplish-brown crab with a hairy covering on its legs while the carapace has few hairs. The fingers of the smooth chelipeds are black and tipped with pale brown. The Smooth-handed Crab ranges from Queensland, around the southern shores to the Swan River in WA. It is common among seagrasses on tidal flats, in estuaries and among rock and wood structures. When disturbed, it will not attempt to try and scuttle away but instead folds its legs tightly under its body and pretends it is a pebble. Males may be parasitised and castrated by a species of shelless barnacle.

Purple Shore Crab *Cyclograpsus granulosus* 20–35mm

This shore crab has a carapace with both the sides and front edge smooth and is broader than it is long. The surface is granular both at the front and sides, hence its species name. The legs are partly flattened, fairly long and strong. Although similar to the **Smooth Shore Crab** (see below) it lacks tufts of long hair between the leg bases. This smooth shore crab has a mottled coloration with varying patterns of brown, purple, red and yellow. This species ranges from Victoria to SA, including Tasmania. It occurs at mid- to high-tide levels on rocky ocean shores, usually under rocks.

Smooth Shore Crab *Cyclograpsus audouinii* 30–40mm

This species has a carapace with smooth rounded edges, without edge spines. The carapace is also more broad than it is long. The chelae are massive, sometimes of unequal size. The hand has a swollen crest on the inner surface. This species may be distinguished from the **Purple Shore Crab** (see above) by having tufts of hair between the bases of the legs. There is great colour variation. Open coast crabs are purple-brown with variable mottled patterns of red-brown, purple and yellow. Estuarine crabs are mottled purple, dark grey or brownish-grey. This species ranges from Hervey Bay in Queensland south to Bunbury in WA. Also found in New Guinea but not Tasmania. It occurs at all tide levels and below, usually sheltering under rocks on rocky and soft bottoms.

Spotted Smooth Shore Crab *Paragrapsus laevis* 30–35mm

This large, often gregarious crab is distinguished by its very large to massive, equal-sized purple-brown and red chelae and its grey or yellow flecked, shiny black carapace. The almost quadrilateral carapace is covered in minute granules and has two distinct edge teeth, while the front has two distinct lobes. The undersurface is creamy yellow. This species ranges from Moreton Bay, Queensland, south to Tasmania. It occurs high on the muddy shores of coastal rivers and estuaries, under pieces of wood, large rocks and boulders, and among debris. It may be very common in mangroves.

Mottled Shore Crab *Paragrapsus gaimardii* 30–35mm

This mid-sized shore crab is similar in form to its northern relative the **Spotted Smooth Shore Crab** (see above). It is distinguished by a shallower notch on the carapace between the eyes and it has a pad of felt only on the underside of the first walking leg, rather than covering the second segment as in

P. laevis. The common names 'mottled' and 'spotted' describe the differences in the carapace blotches. This is a sandy yellow to yellowish-brown crab with dark red mottling over all surfaces. This species ranges from Victoria to SA, overlapping with *P. laevis* in Victoria. It occurs under timber and debris, such as sheets of roofing iron lying on mud shores of rivers and mudflats.

Notched Shore Crab *Paragrapsus quadridentatus* 25–30mm

This attractive mid-sized crab has a grey to pale brown coloured carapace with a green sheen and is marked with dark red spots. The rest of the body and legs are light brown through to cream. The carapace is almost rectangular, slightly broader than long, with a finely granular surface and only slightly convex sides. Although similar to the **Mud Shore Crab** (see below), it has a distinctive projecting tooth on the edge where the sides meet the rear surface. The Notched Shore Crab is restricted to central and western Victoria and Tasmania. It is common on rocky shores and shingle beaches at mid- to low-tide levels on medium- to high-energy shores, often under rocks.

Mud Shore Crab *Helograpsus haswellianus* 25–30mm

This is a medium-sized shore crab with a very deep, smooth carapace. There is a small notch on the carapace behind each orbital (eye) spine. In front of the eye is a stridulating (sound-making) ridge. Mature males have very large claws. The colour is variable, from olive, dark slate-grey to dark chocolate or deep orange. Mature males may have a honey coloured tint, especially on the claws. This species ranges from Pioneer River in Queensland to Port Augusta in SA. It occurs in sheltered bays and estuaries, often well above high-tide levels in mud areas and saltmarsh flats. It shelters under debris or in burrows.

Variegated Shore Crab *Leptograpsus variegatus* 50–80mm

This is an abundant, conspicuous, swift crab found on most non-tropical rocky shores. Its carapace pattern of prominent oblique ridges gives it its other common name, 'Steelback'. It has an almost square carapace, with moderately convex sides. The front of the carapace has many rounded notches. Male chelipeds are very large, with large tubercles on the upper surface of the carpus and claw; female chelipeds are much smaller. The upper segment of the walking legs is expanded and flattened, while the lower three joints are partly spined. There are two quite distinct colour forms,

one purple (see top picture), the other orange (see bottom picture). The eastern form has a purple carapace with lighter flecks or dark steel-grey markings. The southern and western form is orange and has a yellow-green carapace with reddish-yellow markings. In south-west Australia occasional purple-form crabs may be seen among a majority of orange-form crabs. The Variegated Shore Crab ranges from NSW across the southern shores to North West Cape in WA. Tasmania has the purple form on the eastern side and the orange form on the western side. It is also found in New Zealand and South America. It occurs widely over rocky shores to above high-tide levels. Adults shelter in crevices, while juveniles can be found under rock debris. A very tenacious crab, it can cling to rocks being battered by the full force of the waves. If disturbed, it runs quickly sideways to safety. It feeds out in the open, mainly on algae, but it is also a scavenger.

Burrowing Shore Crab *Leptograpsus octodentatus* 45–60mm

This mid-sized crab is found in burrows and rock crevices and under debris, high on sandy shores with medium to high wave action. The carapace has strongly outward-bending (convex) side margins and is covered with low granules. Three sharp teeth (bumps) occur behind each eye-tooth. From these, three grooves extend over the carapace, one quite noticeable. The chelipeds of the male crab are large, while the immovable finger points downward. The crab is olive to purple-brown, with dark brown to yellow mottling. This species ranges from central Victoria to Houtman Abrolhos in WA. It forages at night for dead animals and plant debris, and its sand burrows may be hundreds of metres from the sea. It may have a preference for freshwater seepage.

Grey Shore Crab *Helice leachi* 25–30mm

This dark purple and cream coloured shore crab is round in shape. The chelae in males are very rounded, almost as high as long. The chelae are cream, with purple above. The walking legs are long and slender. Felting is present on the limbs.

This species ranges from Townsville in Queensland south to Sydney. It is found in inlets and bays, not far from a river mouth. It occurs high up on the beach, near high-tide level. It constructs burrows into moderately firm soil, ranging from dirty sand, firm mud to hard-packed earth, among loose shale, stones and mangrove roots.

Red Bait Crab *Plagusia chabrus* 60–70mm

A favourite bait of rock fishermen, this crab could become rare or extinct, if overfished. It is distinguished by its dark red colour, heavily notched front edge, hairy carapace and legs. The hand and carpus of the chelipeds have long rows of coarse tubercles.

Males have larger chelae than females. The first segment of the walking legs is flattened. The rear margins of the legs are armed with spines. The carapace colour is deep red-brown, with pale regions on the walking legs. This species ranges from Newcastle in NSW around the southern shores to Rottnest Island in WA and also occurs in South Africa and South America. It occurs at low-tide levels and below on high-energy rocky shores. It hides under rock ledges, in crevices and among algae.

Sowrie Crab *Plagusia glabra* 50–60mm

This pretty, green coloured crab lives at low-tide levels on rocky shores. The front edge of the carapace is not as notched as the **Red Bait Crab** (see above). There are three distinct, sharp spines on each side of the carapace. The walking legs have sharp spines on the ends, so the Sowrie can grasp rocks. Although appearing green, it is fawn-grey in colour with a covering of dark green spots. Its legs are spotted with brown. This species ranges from south-eastern Queensland to the Victorian border. It prefers to sit at the bottom of rock pools or in cracks and crevices of the rock platform, and appears to live in groups.

Red-fingered Marsh Crab *Sesarma erythrodactyla* 20–30mm

Mature males have an emerald green carapace and orange chelae, with fingers tipped with bright red. The square-shaped carapace is usually greenish-black to nearly black. The green carapace of mature males closely resembles the colour of Grey Mangrove (*Avicennia marina*) seed pods. Immature males and females have much smaller chelae, still tipped with red. This species ranges from central Queensland to southern NSW, with isolated populations in central Victoria and Port Augusta. It is abundant in mangrove swamps, estuarine salt marshes, and on river banks, where it constructs burrows.

Metapograpsus *Metapograpsus latifrons* 40mm

This crossover crab has a square-shaped carapace and is very wide between the eyes. The carapace sides are almost straight but converge partly at the rear. Its colouring is spectacular, with a black carapace, mauve mottling and rich red walking legs and sides to the carapace, merging to white on the chelae fingers. This species ranges from northern WA, across the northern shores to south-eastern Queensland. It occurs under mangroves, often in soft sediment, near high-tide levels, usually under rocks and logs. Its close relative *M. frontalis* (bottom photo) has a black carapace and walking legs specked with light green spots and mauve to white chelae. It has the same distribution range as *M. latifrons* and occurs in similar muddy habitats, as well as under boulders on rocky shores.

59

Common Ghost Crab *Ocypode cordimana* 25–35mm

This common shore crab is seen on open beaches and sandy shores in estuaries. Its body is rectangular, slightly more broad than long. The eyestalks are without terminal tips. Males are slightly larger than females but in both sexes one chelae is much larger than the other. A translucent, cream-coloured crab, it is often tinged with yellow or pink. This species ranges from the Kimberley in northern WA, across the northern shores to the central NSW coast. It digs deep burrows in dry sand near estuary entrances and in sandhills backing ocean beaches. Burrows may be hundreds of metres from the shore, up to 1m deep. It forages at night for food on the shoreline.

Horn-eyed Ghost Crab *Ocypode ceratopthalma* 45–50mm

This swift-running, buff-white and chocolate-brown coloured crab has distinctive long extensions on the top of its eyes in adults. Rectangular in shape, it has large, unequal-sized chelae. There is a rasping ridge on the inside palm of the claw. The male rubs this ridge against the sides of its carapace to create a scratching sound, which is used to defend its territory. This species ranges from Shark Bay in WA, across the northern shores to southern NSW. It is widespread in tropical parts of the Indian and Pacific oceans. It is found in burrows just above high-tide level on ocean and sandy estuarine beaches. These crabs emerge at night to feed on flotsam left by the tide.

Western Ghost Crab *Ocypode convexa* 40–45mm

This large, distinctive, golden-coloured ghost crab has a deep, square, robust body and strong running and digging legs. Its eyestalks do not have a terminal spike, like the **Horn-eyed Ghost Crab** (see page 60). Although it has a rasping ridge on the inside of the claws, it has not been recorded as making sound. Males are slightly larger and have larger chelae than females. This species is found only between Bunbury and Exmouth Gulf in WA. It occurs on sandy ocean beaches in burrows at high-tide levels, sometimes a short distance from the water. Where the **Common Ghost Crab**, (see page 60) and this species occur together at North West Cape, the Western Ghost Crab occurs higher up on the beach, in drier areas.

Semaphore Crab *Heloecius cordiformis* 20–25mm

An equal-handed, almost barrel-shaped crab with light purple chelae and white fingers. The carapace is mottled dark purple; the purple eyestalks are held upright. The young look different from the adults. Their purple carapace is mottled with light grey, and their chelae are light orange-red, making it easy to confuse them with the **Red-fingered Marsh Crab** (see page 59), which occurs in the same areas. The Sephamore Crab ranges from southern Queensland to Tasmania and is found in large groups in estuaries where there is a soft but stable mudflat. It digs a vertical burrow, usually near mangroves. The waving pattern of the male's chelae is distinctive. When disturbed, these crabs race toward a protective burrow.

Seagrass Sentinel Crab *Macropthalmus crassipes* 30–40mm

The carapace of this thick-set, rectangular-shaped crab is twice as wide as it is long. The carapace is drab green with light brown chelae. Long eyestalks occupy the whole width of the front. Unlike other crabs in its genus, the chelipeds of the males are equal in size. A bump on the lower fixed finger of the chelae is distinctive. When threatened or in display, both chelae are raised. This species ranges from northern WA across the northern shores to NSW. Males are territorial and will repulse competitors with a ritualised display. It occurs in seagrass meadows of estuaries.

Mudflat Sentinel Crab *Macropthalmus setosus* 30–40mm

This is a rectangular-shaped crab with a carapace twice as wide as it is long but flatter than the **Seagrass Sentinel Crab** (see above). It has very long eyestalks, occupying the whole width of the front. The chelae of mature males are light blue. To distinguish this crab from *M. crassipes*, look for a bump on the movable upper finger of the chelae instead of on the lower fixed finger. This species ranges from eastern Queensland to Sydney. It is often seen feeding at low-tide on most estuarine muddy shores. It will lie partly buried in sloppy mud in shallow pools, with only its long eyestalks appearing above the water surface.

Southern Sentinel Crab *Macrophthalmus latifrons* 25mm

The Southern Sentinel Crab's eyes are not as tall as those of its northern relatives, being only one-third the width of carapace. The eye orbits occupy the entire front carapace margin, apart from the frontal section. The crab's carapace width is 1.5 times its length. Its surface is covered with fine granules. The chelae's immovable finger points downward, and both chelae fingers curve inward for scooping up detritus. The walking legs are fringed with long hairs and dense patches of fur are on the second and third pairs of legs. The crab is yellowish-brown and is found on sand and mudflats of Victoria and SA, where it burrows among the seagrasses. It was formerly called *Hemiplax latifrons*.

Sand Bubbler Crab *Scopimera inflata* 12mm

The squat, compact Sand Bubbler Crab is similar in shape to the ghost crabs but is much smaller. The chelae are equal sized. A male's chelae are larger than a female's. A flattened membrane occurs on the inner surface (merus) of each leg. This crab is sand-coloured and well camouflaged. This species ranges from Exmouth Gulf in WA, across northern shores to Port Stephens in NSW, and occurs on sheltered sandy ocean beaches and bays, in vertical burrows at high-tide levels. When feeding, it makes a very characteristic pattern of small pellets of sand, radiating out from the burrow. It feeds on organic material sifted out from the sand pellets by its mouthparts.

Compressed Fiddler Crab *Uca coarctata* 20–30mm

This beautiful fiddler crab has a dark carapace and a distinctive rust-red to orange cheliped that grades to dull orange-grey and grey-cream. The eyestalks are grey-brown, the legs grey-brown with some cream. Males have a white patch on the hind walking legs. This species ranges from Darwin, NT, east and south to Moreton Bay and the Gold Coast in southern Queensland. It prefers to be high up on steep banks where it lives above *Uca polita* and below *Uca dussumieri*, two other fiddler crabs. On more gently sloping mudflats, it is found with **Long-digit Uca** (see page 65) and *Uca vocans*.

Flamed Fiddler Crab *Uca flammula* 20–30mm

This brilliantly coloured fiddler crab is very distinctive. It has a black carapace with some orange and the major cheliped of the adult male is orange to orange-red. The eyestalks are pale purple-pink and the legs are orange-red. Females may have black on the high part of the walking legs. Young adults are usually brown with

orange-yellow chelae. This species ranges from Exmouth Gulf in WA, across the northern shores to the Gulf of Carpentaria in Queensland. It occurs on the muddy upper banks of steeply banked creeks. It is usually found above *Uca polita* and below *Uca parvo*.

Distinctive Fiddler Crab *Uca signata* 20–25mm

Males of this species have a dull blue-green carapace with white marbling. The main cheliped is grey to white, with red-brown and grey-blue parts to the arms. The eyestalks are orange-brown, while the legs are brown to blue-grey. The mouthparts are brown-blue with a white band. This species ranges from Derby, northern WA, across the northern shores to Maryborough and Gladstone in Queensland. It is found on sandy mud on the upper levels of gently sloping creek banks. It may be found with the **Flamed Fiddler Crab** or with the **Compressed Fiddler Crab** (both on page 64).

Long-digit Uca *Uca longidigita* 20–30mm

The carapace is turquoise-blue with brown and cream markings. Adult males have three black diamond markings on the carapace. The major cheliped of males is a pale grey-blue and white, with a touch of orange on the inner face. The eyestalks are grey-black, the legs dark grey-black. This species is found at Green Island in Moreton Bay as well as the Brisbane River, Queensland. It occurs on banks of tidal rivers and in mud to sandy mud along the ocean side of mangroves. Occurs with the **Compressed Fiddler Crab** (see page 64) and the **Orange-clawed Fiddler Crab** (see page 66).

Orange-clawed Fiddler Crab *Uca vomeris* 20–30mm

The brilliant orange-coloured chelae of the male in this widespread fiddler crab are conspicuous. Males have one chela much larger than the other. The female has equal-sized chelae. Specimens from northern Australia are more brightly coloured than southern examples. This species ranges from Darwin in the NT and around the eastern shores south as far as Sydney. It occurs on unshaded sandy mud at the lower tide levels of open bays and creeks. The orange chelae of the males look like brightly coloured decaying leaves, waving on the mudflat. The ritualistic waving of the chelae is to repel other males and attract females.

Canary-yellow Clawed Fiddler Crab *Uca mjobergi* 20–30mm

This fiddler crab, with a canary-yellow cheliped, has a deep body, with a carapace wider than it is long. The carapace is grey-brown with some white mottling. In males, it feels smooth but looks microscopically granular, while the female's carapace looks and feels microscopically granular. Males have a distinctive canary-yellow major

cheliped. The front surfaces of a male's walking legs are orange. The legs are grey with brown and white speckling, occasionally banded. The eyestalks are grey-brown and fairly thick. This species ranges from Carnarvon in WA, across northern Australia to Gove in the NT. It occurs on sand to sandy mud shores on the landward side of mangroves in sheltered estuaries, bays and river entrances.

Lemon-yellow Clawed Fiddler Crab *Uca perplexa* 15–20mm

This beautiful lemon-yellow-coloured fiddler crab is found way above high-tide levels on sandy shores. Its carapace is grey-black with some cream mottling. The major chelae and fingers are lemon-yellow, with some grey-yellow. The eyestalks are grey-black, while the legs have brown and grey banding, occasionally with some grey speckles. The mouth region is pale grey. This species ranges from Cape York in far northern Queensland, south to Trial Bay and Red Rock in NSW. It is found high on sand to sandy mud shores on both the landward and seaward edge of mangrove regions in sheltered bays, creeks and river mouths.

Pea Crab *Pinnotheres hickmani* 10mm female

This is a small, globular crab, with no sculpture, and its abdomen is very large, soft and smooth. The tiny eyes are not visible from above. The chelipeds are small, weak and equal-sized but still stronger than the somewhat spindly legs. Females are much larger than males and they are pale cream, fawn to dark brown in colour while those bearing eggs are darker. This species ranges from central Victoria across the southern shores to Shark Bay in WA and is usually found in inlets and bays. Females live inside the bodies of other animals, such as in the mantle of bivalve molluscs, especially the **Edible Mussel** (see page 122), in sea urchins and some univalve molluscs. The male is free-swimming.

Light Blue Soldier Crab *Mictyris longicarpus* 12–15mm

This light blue and white globe-shaped crab has a distinctive dark patch on each joint of its spindly legs. These crabs form large armies on sandy areas of estuaries and headlands. When feeding, they leave small round pellets of sand behind. Soldier crabs can walk straight ahead, while all other crabs walk sideways.

Large groups may erupt in a horde when the tide reaches a certain low level. If disturbed, they burrow into the damp sand with a corkscrew motion. This species ranges from Shark Bay in WA, across northern Australia and down to eastern Victoria.

Dark Blue Soldier Crab *Mictyris platycheles* 12–15mm

This distinctive, globe-shaped, dark blue and grey soldier crab has prominent purple and white side bulges, long thin legs and flattened chelipeds. It does not have dark patches on leg joints like the **Light Blue Soldier Crab** (see above). This species ranges from Moreton

Bay in Queensland, south to Port Phillip Bay in Victoria and Tasmania. It occurs in estuaries where sandflats are gradually becoming mudflats. It forms large feeding groups only on southern shores. Its relative, the Light Blue Soldier Crab, is more common on northern shores. Large amounts of sand are processed to extract micro-algae and detritus food. The processed sand is left as round pellets. If disturbed, the Dark Blue Soldier Crab rapidly burrows into sediment in a spiral manner.

Australian Chiton *Ischnochiton australis* 70–90mm

This large, flat, oval chiton has a medium-width girdle sculptured with large, thick, keeled, pebble-like scales. The end valves have strong irregular radiating ribs, while the lateral areas have diagonal ribs. The central valves are longitudinally ribbed. The shell segments (valves) and girdle are dark green to greenish-brown, rarely blue. The side areas are brown and the middle and side areas are green with brown flecks. This species ranges from southern Queensland, around the south-eastern shores to the Great Australian Bight, in SA. It occurs under rocks on reefs and rocky shores at low-tide level and below to 8m on high-energy coasts. If disturbed, it will curl up and drop into the water.

Elongated Chiton *Ischnochiton elongatus* 25–35mm

This is a medium-sized, oval shaped, longish chiton, usually with a dark coloured background and a pale stripe along its centre. Its front shell segment and side areas have fine, radiating, noduled ribs. Bordering the front are fine, irregular radiating rows of fine bumps overlying a finer sculpture. The snakeskin-like girdle scales are medium-sized, uniform, round-oval and striated. Apart from the common form, other colours include olive, green, grey, brown, black, blue, purple, red or cream, with various dots, stripes or wavy lines. This species ranges from NSW, around the southern shores to Shark Bay in WA. It occurs at the lowest tide levels and below to 10m, on sheltered to moderately exposed shores, usually under boulders embedded in sand.

Variegated Ischnochiton *Ischnochiton versicolor* 60–65mm

A large, beautifully coloured, elongate and oval chiton. Its end valves and side areas have strong, flat, crowded, radial ribs. The front valve is smaller than the end valve. The side areas have three or four wavy ridges that become finer and more zigzagged in the middle region. The girdle scales are large, rounded, oval and striated with six to eight grooves. Colour is variable, with green, black, brown, blue, rose and white base colours and markings. It is impossible to describe all the colour variations. This species ranges from NSW, around the southern shores to SA, including Tasmania. It occurs at mid-tide levels and below on open and semi-protected areas, under stones.

Jewelled Chiton *Acanthopleura gemmata* 80–100mm

This large, coarse chiton is variable in shape and height, with distinctive long calcareous spines on the girdle. It has a shell sculpture of blister-like bumps. The front and rear valves have multiple slits, while the middle valve has one slit. The shell valves have well-developed insertion plates with comb-like teeth that hold the adjacent valves together. The shell colour is brown or greenish-grey, with black marks on the jugium (valve peak). The shell is usually eroded. The spined girdle is banded black and white. This species ranges from central WA, across the northern shores to northern Queensland. It occurs at high-tide levels and below in crevices or exposed on rocks.

Spiculed Chiton *Acanthopleura gaimardi* 60mm

Although its eight shell plates are plain, this chiton is distinguished by its black-and-brown banded girdle, which consists of numerous, pointed to blunt conical spinelets. The anterior valve and side areas are sculptured with low, inconspicuous granules in ill-defined radial rows. The central area of the valves is featureless, except for a hump in the second-last valve. The end valve is flat and triangular. The valves are dull greenish-brown, with lighter grey areas, eroding to almost white. This species ranges from northern Queensland to southern NSW shores. It occurs out in the open on exposed rock surfaces at mid-tide level and below, and is confined to the tidal region.

Hairy Chiton *Acanthopleura hirtosa* 50–60mm

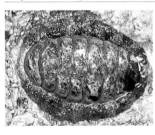

This is a large, flattened, oval, black- to brown-coloured chiton. It has a distinctive black-and-white girdle, with short, conical, 'club-head' scales. The shell sculpture is of weak tubercles, usually detected only in juveniles and protected individuals because most adults are eroded. The front valve has ten slits,

while the middle valve has one slit and the end valve is calloused. All the valve insertion plates have comb-like teeth to keep the valves in line. This species occurs in WA, where it is common at mid- to low-tide levels and below on limestone reefs and shores. It is usually found in protective gutters and hollows.

71

Snake-skin Chiton *Chiton pelliserpentis* 63–65mm

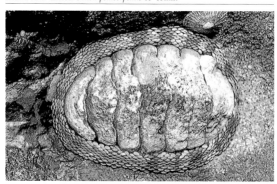

This common, large, oval and elongated chiton, is distinguished by having a girdle that looks like snake skin. The girdle scales are large, oval and marked with close striations. The shell valves have a sharp ridge called a keel. This chiton is often eroded. Shell colour is green to blackish-brown, with a black second valve. Other valve tips are black. The girdle has alternating bands of black and grey. This species ranges along the east coast, including NSW to Tasmania, as well as New Zealand. It occurs at mid-tide level and below on intertidal rocks, preferring cracks, crevices and gutters to retain moisture and avoid the sun.

White Plaxiphora Chiton *Plaxiphora albida* 40–100mm

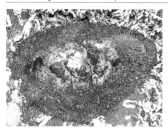

This large, oval, humped chiton may be found quite high on the shore, sometimes at the highest tide levels. The shell is dark green to brown, marked with cream or yellow wavy bars. The shell segments (valves) have a white-tipped beak on the front edge. The

wide, leathery girdle has long bristles, often eroded in larger chitons. The girdle is brown with darker bars, and the foot is bright red. This species lives intertidally, often on exposed rock surfaces, and ranges from southern Queensland around the southern shores to southern WA. It shows homing behaviour, returning to the same location after a feeding journey.

Yellow Chiton *Onithochiton quercinus* 80mm

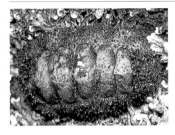

This chiton has a low, flat valve, covered by wavy markings, and a wide, leathery girdle that appears smooth. Coloration is variable. The shell plates are nearly always eroded. The girdle is really covered with minute spicules, too small to be seen with the naked eye.

The rows of black spots across the valves are light-sensitive organs called ocelli or shell eyes. This species has a split distribution. The eastern form ranges from Mackay in Queensland to southern NSW. The western form ranges from Esperance to the Houtman Abrolhos in WA. It occurs at mid-tide level and below on horizontal rock surfaces over which the surf rolls, in cracks and gutters or in pools.

Mysterious Chiton *Cryptoplax mystica* 120mm

This chiton is long, brown and worm-like, with an extremely large girdle and small separate valves. Although the valves are in contact in juveniles, they grow apart in adults. The valves are sculptured with coarse blister-like bumps or crumpled wavy lines. This chiton is able to bend to match its habitat. In large specimens, the shell valves are so small that they seem to disappear. Most of the upper surface is a fleshy girdle, with small spines. The colour ranges from fawn to orange. The species appears to be restricted to NSW, where it is found under stones at and below low-tide level.

73

Common Earshell or Abalone *Haliotis rubra* 100–125mm

The edible abalone is large and oval, with a greatly enlarged body whorl. It is sculptured with weak growth ridges, over irregular oblique radiating folds. Around the shell edge is a row of conical tubercles, with six or seven open for respiration. Inside

the shell are oblique wrinkles. Shell colour is reddish-brown, with narrow, curved, radiating light green streaks. Inside the shell is brightly iridescent. This species ranges from northern NSW, around the southern shores to southern WA. It occurs at and below low-tide levels on rocky shores. It is found under rocks, in crevices, in caves or on vertical rock faces.

Scarlet-rayed Abalone *Haliotis coccoradiata* 30–50mm

This abalone shell is ear-shaped, oval, rather thin, narrowing anteriorly, with a low spire. It has a flat dorsal surface, sculptured with numerous irregular concentric ridges crossed by fine longitudinal striations. On the side of the shell are three

sharp spiral ridges with smooth interspaces. The respiratory holes are very slightly raised, round, with six or seven open. The shell exterior is reddish-brown with broad, irregular, radiating, curved cream rays. The spire is pink. The shell interior is silvery, with a pink and green sheen. The animal is light green, with darker markings. This species ranges from northern NSW to Mallacoota in Victoria. It appears to be a common species found at the lowest tide levels and below.

Elephant Snail *Scutus antipodes* 70–150mm

This is the largest of the Australian false limpets, easily identified because the large animal is tough and jet-black in colour. Folds of mantle almost conceal the oval, whitish coloured shell. The shell is large, solid and shield-shaped.

Unlike other false limpets, there is no oval perforation or slit and no bold sculpture. This species ranges from NSW, around the southern shores to Geraldton in WA, including Tasmania and also New Zealand. It occurs commonly in rocky pools and crevices, often under rocks and boulders at low-tide levels and below to 20m, on rocky ocean shores. It is an active algal feeder, moving quickly when disturbed.

Scutus *Scutus unguis* 40–45mm

The body of this Scutus is large and fleshy, with a large flattened shell, its peaked apex at about one-third of its length from the anterior end and points forward. The anal notch is V-shaped, wide and shallow. The sculpture is of faint concentric striations,

like small pustules. The animal has a slug-like appearance, where the body folds up around the edge of the shell. The body colour is light- to mid-brown, with a white to fawn shell. This species ranges from Shark Bay in WA across the northern shores to southern Queensland. It is found at low-tide levels and below on rocky shores, lightly covered with a mud layer. Also called *S. granulatus*, *S. olonguis* and *S. dunguis*.

Black Keyhole Limpet *Amblychilepas nigrita* 10–20mm

The shell is oblong-oval, flattened, with raised front and rear edges. The animal is twice as long as the shell. The oval 'keyhole', with a distinct, thickened rim, is just behind the shell middle. The sculpture is of many fine, radial ribs, crossed by concentric growth ridges that form a lace pattern. The white or bluish-shell interior is smooth, with pale brown rays. The exterior is brown, grey or fawn, with irregular rays of dark brown. The animal is pink to pale brown. This species ranges from NSW, around the southern shores to WA. It occurs at mid- to low-tide levels and below on exposed and semi-protected rocky shores, often under rocks and stones.

Diodora *Diodora lineata* 40–55mm

This distinctive keyhole limpet is distinguished by its oval to rectangular-shaped shell. It has a high apex with a round hole at the peak, a sculpture of 20 primary radial ribs and two or three minor ribs between, crossed by oval concentric ridges to produce a latticed effect. The shell margin is faintly crenulated. The hole is for excreting metabolic wastes and there is no operculum. The shell exterior is yellowish-white, blotched brown or with radial stripes. Inside the shell is white. This species ranges from southern Queensland south to Port Phillip Bay in Victoria. It occurs under stones at low-tide levels to exposed rocky shores. Unlike other slit limpets, it is able to conceal itself under its shell.

False Limpet *Clypidina rugosa* 15–20mm

The small, oval and cone-shaped shell is identified by its distinctive ribs, granular structure and a small hind slit. The apex is near the centre, leaning toward the front. It is sculptured with 12–15 strong radial ribs, with two or three smaller ribs between the larger ribs. They are all crossed by concentric ridges, forming a granular appearance. The shell's white interior is smooth, except for a distinct groove from the apex to the notch at the shell hind end. Its external colour is greyish-brown or white when eroded. This species ranges from southern Queensland, around the southern shores to southern WA. It occurs at all tidal levels, and is often associated with *Galeolaria* tubes, mussels or Cunjevoi.

Scaly Limpet *Patella peronii* 35–40mm

This large, tall, solid, oval, cone-shaped limpet has up to 24 prominent ribs that extend to form a notched margin. The upper surface is roughened by a covering of scales. Shell colour is dull white, with white ribs marked brown or black in the spaces. Inside the shell is lacquer-white with an orange-yellow tinge at apex (spatula). The spatula margin is often rimmed black. This species ranges from central NSW, around the southern shores to southern WA, including Tasmania. It is found at low-tide levels and below on exposed rock platforms. It is often found among kelp holdfasts. Fish such as wrasses eat this limpet. It spawns in late summer in NSW.

Chapman's Limpet *Helcion chapmani* 15–20mm

This limpet has a distinctive shell with eight radiating ribs. Rough surf examples have distinct ribs and a very irregular margin, while those from more sheltered locations have indistinct ribs and are more oval. The shell is marked with very fine radiating lines. Exterior colour is reddish-brown, while the interior is white with a pink tint. It

is distributed in NSW, Tasmania and SA but is rare in Victoria. It occurs at the very lowest tide levels on rocky shores and is not often found alive. This species must be very common on ocean reefs as its shells are very frequently washed up on beaches. Also known as *Patella chapmani*.

Giant Limpet *Patella laticostata* 90–110mm

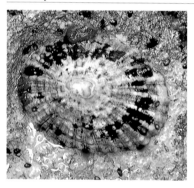

This is the largest Australian limpet. The shell is solid, oval-shaped, conical and quite tall. it is sculptured with numerous radiating ribs and riblets of varying size and widths. Shell margin is finely crenulated, with groups of two to four longer teeth-like bumps around the inner surface. The exterior is green-

ish-grey with white ribs and brownish interspaces. The porcellaneous interior is brown or fawn. The edge of the shell is conspicuously marked with paired dark blotches. The distribution of this species is limited to WA, between Esperance and Shark Bay. It occurs at all tidal levels on rocky ocean shores of southern WA. Giant Limpets often have one or more small limpets, *Patelloida nigrosulcata*, attached to their shells in a commensal relationship.

Variegated Limpet *Cellana tramoserica* 50-60mm

The is the most common limpet at mid-tide level in south-eastern Australia. There is a great variation in colour and form, hence its common name. The eastern and southern colour forms are so different, they could easily be mistaken for separate species. Eastern forms (top photo) have a conspicuous radial banding of many colours, including brown, black, orange, yellow, pink and white. Usually every third of fourth rib is darker, creating a striped pattern. Southern forms (bottom photo) are almost monotone, being light brown with a fine, speckled pattern.

Both forms are oval-shaped, slightly broader at the rear. The apex is not quite central. and the sculpture is of 36 strong, radial ribs with many fine, encircling close growth lines. The margin is finely scalloped. Those found low on the shore may be quite wide, thick and tall. High on the shore, they may be quite flat and thin-shelled. This species ranges from southern Queensland to eastern SA, including eastern Tasmania. It occurs across all tide levels from the high-water mark down, most commonly at mid-tide levels. It can tolerate a wide range of habitats and is found under many conditions of exposure and dampness. It has the ability to excavate a depression for itself in the rock and exhibits 'homing' behaviour.

Orange-edged Limpet *Cellana solida* 60–80mm

This large, strikingly coloured, orange-edged limpet is found along South Australian shores. Oval-shaped and flattened, it has a deeply scalloped margin and 21–37 broad radiating ribs coarsely grooved by distinct concentric growth lines. The shell may be eroded. The exterior is dull grey to buff with brown radial rays and a distinctive orange margin blotched with reddish-brown. The interior is silvery nacreous, with a bluish-yellow to golden tinge. The animal is olive green, with a bluish-brown foot and speckled olive tentacles. This species ranges between western Victoria and Tasmania to the Great Australian Bight in SA. It is common on rocks at high- to mid-tidal levels and below.

Rainbow Limpet *Cellana conciliata* 35mm

An oval limpet-shaped shell with a low, near central apex. The sculpture is of numerous, very small, delicate, evenly sized radiating riblets. The margin is very weakly scalloped. Exterior is dull grey to white with indistinct brown to black markings, while the interspaces are light brown. The interior is silvery blue to cream or white, with radial light lines around the shell margin. This species is similar to the **Variegated Limpet** (see page 79), but with a sculpture of numerous very fine radial riblets. This species ranges from north-eastern Queensland to mid-eastern Queensland. It occurs in the mid- to low-tide regions on rocky shores protected by the Great Barrier Reef.

Tall-ribbed Limpet *Patelloida alticostata* 25–40mm

This distinctive, solid, cone-shaped limpet has 12–30 (usually 18) strong, partly scaled ribs, creating a notched shell margin. It is dull white to grey-green with fine crescent-shaped brown marks in the rib spaces forming a cobweb pattern. It is often eroded. This species ranges from northern NSW, around the southern coastline up to Geraldton in WA. It occurs at and below low-tide level on exposed rocky coasts. It feeds on algae and often shelters among red coralline seaweeds. It takes six days for the yellow-coloured mature oocyte (egg) to grow into a young, crawling animal.

Lateral-striped Limpet *Patelloida latistrigata* 12–20mm

This small, oval, cone-shaped limpet shell has a sculpture of irregular, rounded ribs with several major rays, interspersed with 12–15 minor ribs. The shell colour is dark brown, with dark rays on the ribs. The interior is bluish-white with a dark brown margin. The spatula is brown, spotted with blue or brown, bordered with white at the end of the ribs. This species ranges from southern Queensland to eastern SA. It lives at mid- to high-tide levels on exposed rocks or in holes and crevices, washed by medium- to high-energy waves. It is often found among barnacles and *Siphonaria diemenensis, S. funiculata* and *Notoacmea granulosa*. It breeds throughout summer.

Cryptic Limpet *Patelloida cryptalirata* 12mm

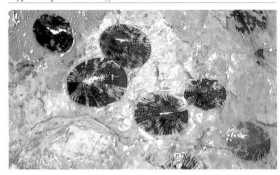

The Cryptic Limpet's shell shape is a thin, low elliptic oval, with its apex at the anterior third and its front and rear slopes straight or slightly convex. The shell surface is smooth with no sculpture. The exterior is cream or light brown with a reticulated pattern of fine red-brown lines that may form wide radial bands or a wide cross. Inside the shell is white or brown with a blue-tinged marginal band. The spatula is brown. This species ranges from Broome in WA across the northern shores to southern Queensland. It occurs on tropical rocky shores, often sheltering in rock crevices or under stones in protected areas.

Star Limpet *Patelloida saccharina stella* 22–25mm

The Star Limpet's shell has a long oval shape, sometimes narrower at the rear, with a pronounced sculpture of 18–20 strong, high, uneven radial ribs, sticking out to form a star-like pattern. The apex is nearly central. The colour is greyish, with dark grey to brown between the high ribs. There are occasional V-shaped lines near the shell margin. The shell interior is white, with an olive-green, yellow or white horseshoe-shaped spatula, finely dotted with brown. The margin is spotted or rimmed with black. This species ranges from North West Cape in WA across the northern shores to southern Queensland. It occurs on rocky shores in the mid- to low-tidal regions, sometimes in exposed situations.

Granulated Limpet *Collisella mixta* 15–23mm

This is a tall limpet, solid, thick and oval, with its apex one-third from the front, often with a 'Maltese cross' marking. The front slope is convex, while the rear slope is steep and almost straight. The shell surface is finely granular, with a sculpture of many irregular, often eroded, flat radial ribs. Shell colour is grey to yellow or fawn, marked with dark brown rays. The interior is bluish-white with a dark brown margin, spatula and markings. This species ranges from Lakes Entrance in Victoria to southern SA, but is rare in Tasmania. It lives at high- to mid-tide levels on exposed rocky shore platforms, usually in holes and crevices.

Banded Limpet *Collisella onychitis* 15–20mm

This limpet's shell is oval, thick, narrow at the rear, sculptured with about 20 radial ribs, either weak or strong, growing closer to the rear. The shell margin is thin and notched. The shell is often eroded, which obliterates the sculpture. It is a variable species in colour, shape and sculpture. Its colour is white, cream or grey with brown radial rays. The spaces between the ribs are dark brown, often flecked with white. Inside the shell is white and porcellaneous, with a light brown spatula and white muscle scar. Heavily eroded shells are very dark. This species ranges from Ceduna in SA to the Murchison River in WA and occurs at low-tide levels and below, on rocks.

Tall Limpet *Notoacmea alta* 10–15mm

This small limpet (the small brown one in the photo) has a fragile shell, with a characteristic high, cone-shaped apex at one end. The surface is smooth, with very fine radial and concentric striations. The outside is very dark brown or black, with occasional dull white to light green bands radiating from the apex. Inside the shell is chocolate brown with radiating lighter bands. This species ranges from southern NSW to Spencer Gulf in SA, including eastern Tasmania. This limpet lives at mid- to low-tide levels, often attached to other shells, such as the **Beaked Mussel** (see page 123).

May's Beetle Limpet *Notoacmea mayi* 15–20mm

This small, oval and flattened limpet has a distinctively positioned shell apex that may extend to — or past — the front edge of the shell. It has a lack of shell markings and its colour varies, ranging from light brown to grey mottled with darker browns or greys. The interior of the shell is also variable in colour, ranging from chestnut to dark brown with a black spatula, while the inside shell margin is spotted with black and yellow. This species ranges from western Victoria to eastern SA and Tasmania. It occurs on vertical rock faces up to high-tide levels.

Flamed Limpet *Notoacmea flammea* 18–22mm

The shell of this limpet is small, oval, thin and conical. The sculpture is of very fine, radial lines and concentric striations that intersect to form characteristic well-spaced, beaded riblets. Its apex is toward the front. Colour is variable, ranging from cream to black with brown markings that form a cross or flamed pattern. The shell interior is also variable, usually white to bluish with a dark border. This species ranges from central NSW, around the southern shores to Perth in WA. It occurs at low-tide levels in pools and protected areas, under stones or on pool walls. This is a variable species or species complex, which has been given many scientific names.

Petterd's Limpet *Notoacmea petterdi* 12–20mm

This is a well-camou-flaged, small- to medium-sized, flattened, oval limpet with a sharp apex at the rear quarter and an arched base slope. The sculpture is of widely spaced, smooth riblets crossed by concentric growth lines. The shell colour ranges from a dull white to light brown, marked with 30–40 dark

brown radiating bands. The shell interior is pale brown with an apex of chocolate brown. This species ranges from Southern Queensland, south to eastern SA, including Tasmania. A common, cryptic limpet, it is often found in groups, at or near high-tide levels on vertical rock surfaces exposed to ocean spray.

Rounded False Ear Shell *Granata imbricata* 25–35mm

This mollusc looks like a small abalone but lacks the respiratory holes around the shell. The shell is rounded, solid and ear-shaped with a greatly enlarged body whorl and large aperture. Unlike the similar **Elongate False Ear Shell** (see below), the shell completely covers this animal's body parts. Its sculpture is of numerous spiral riblets covered with fine scales. The operculum is extremely small and apparently functionless. Colour is cream to light brown outside with irregular reddish-brown dots; inside is a silvery iridescent nacre. This species ranges from southern Queensland around the southern shores to southern WA. It occurs under rocks and boulders at and below low-tide level and in pools and gutters on rocky ocean shores.

Elongate False Ear Shell *Stomatella impertusa* 22–25mm

This fragile, flattened, oblong- or ear-shaped shell has a single, large body whorl with a large aperture. The sculpture is of fine oblique striations. Although the animal lies within the wide, flared mouth of the shell, much of its foot is exposed and cannot be retracted into the shell. If molested, it can break off the rear part of its foot; this can

be regrown later. Colour is variable and includes pink, slate-grey, mauve or black, with stripes, spots or streaks of other colours. This species ranges from NSW, around the southern shores to Kalbarri in WA, including Tasmania. It may occur in groups at low-tide levels or in pools, often under rocks on sheltered to moderately exposed reef. Also known as *Gena impertusa*.

Conical Thalotia *Thalotia conica* 15–20mm

This is a small, solid, conical shell with slightly rounded whorls. The sculpture is of granular, spiral ribs — around six on the whorls and six on the base. The aperture is small and squarish, with a thick and sharp outer lip marked with several nodules. The operculum is round and horny. The exterior is reddish-brown to pink with dark brown flecked spiral ribs. Whitish axial lines form a tessellated appearance. The apex is red, crimson or pink. This species ranges from Wilsons Promontory in Victoria across the southern shores to Geraldton in WA. It is mostly found in estuaries on seagrasses. On ocean shores it is found on algae growing in rock pools or on seagrass in sheltered areas.

Lined Trochus *Trochus lineatus* 50mm

This is a strongly conical shell with a circular base. The straight sides form a sharp edge with the sometimes concave base. The columella is smooth or with many faint bumps. The sculpture is of granular spiral lines and lengthened, oblique, nodules widely spaced on the lower part of the whorls. The base has fine spiral lines. The

shell is cream to green with red oblique lines, occasionally with red sides. The base is patterned with thin, wavy, radiating lines. This species ranges from the Houtman Abrolhos in WA, across the northern shores to southern Queensland. It is very common on coral reefs and rocky shore habitats.

Zebra Top Shell *Austrocochlea porcata* 25mm

This is the common zebra-striped, ribbed top shell. The shell is conical and globe-shaped, with a sharp apex. It is similar in shape to the **Ribbed Top Shell** (see below) and until recently, the two have been considered to be one species. The Zebra Top Shell is distinguished by its less tall, broken spiral ridges and the oblique black-and-white banded pattern overlying the light grey to white shell. This species ranges from Townsville in Queensland, around the southern shores to Geraldton in WA. It often occurs in large numbers at mid-tide level and below on rocky ocean shores, especially in moist areas, in rock pools and in estuaries. It is very common in south-eastern Australia.

Ribbed Top Shell *Austrocochlea constricta* 25–50mm

The shell is thick and conical, with a sharp apex. The distinctive rounded whorls are sculptured with five or six strong spiral ribs, which creates a grooved appearance. The shell height is equal to its width. The aperture is rounded and ridged and the columella is short, with a single tooth. The operculum is horny and round. Colour is a uniform dull grey to off-white. This species ranges from Coffs Harbour in NSW, around the southern shores to Albany in WA. It is abundant at mid-tide levels on exposed rock surfaces on medium- to low-energy shores. It feeds on algae, which it rasps off the bases of rock pools.

Wavy Top Shell *Austrocochlea concamerata* 20–25mm

The Wavy Top Shell is distinguished by its flatter shell, greater number of ribs and yellow spotted or streaked interior. Its shell is wider than high, being thick, round and conical. Its sculpture is of many spiral ribs. Shell colour is black and marked with yellow spots. The lip edge is marked with black and yellow. Inside the shell, including the columella, is white. The operculum is round. This species ranges from NSW around the southern shores to the Houtman Abrolhos in WA. It is found at mid- to high-tide levels on exposed rock surfaces on medium- to high-energy shores. Locally abundant, it lives in groups and hides in cracks or under rock ledges.

Checkered Top Shell *Austrocochlea odontis* 15–18mm

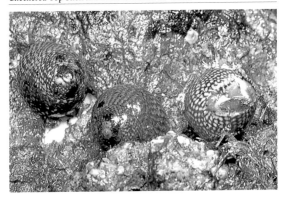

This solid, globe-shaped, univalve mollusc, is easily recognised by its distinctive light spots and green interior. The shell is either smooth or marked with very fine grooves. Shell colour is dark grey to bluish-black, with numerous yellowish-white markings in a checkered pattern. The edge of the aperture is black. The shell interior is green, while the columella edge is bright green. There is a faint tooth on the columella. The brown operculum is round. This species ranges from Waratah Bay in Victoria to SA, including Tasmania. It is commonly found at and below mid-tide level on algae and under stones in rock pools.

89

Smooth Top Shell *Austrocochlea rudis* 35–40mm

The Smooth Top Shell (top right) is solid and turban-shaped with a high spire. Its exterior is smooth; height and width are about equal. Inside the aperture are narrow, angled ridges. Small raised points (teeth) occur on the lip line. The shell colour is dark purple-grey with a dark green to black lip. This species ranges from SA to the Murchison River in WA. It is common to abundant at mid- to low-tide levels on rocky shores. The species appears to be a south-west equivalent of the **Zebra Top Shell** and **Ribbed Top Shell** (see both on page 88), which are abundant in south-eastern Australia.

Top Shell *Monodonta labio* 30–35mm

A solid, cone-shaped shell with a sculpture of strong, granular ribs, a moderately high spire and a flattened base. The outer lip is toothed on the inner margin. The columella has a large, square tooth. Base colour is grey, brown, green or red, with darker granules. It has a periostracum covering, nacreous

beneath. This species ranges from Shark Bay in WA across the northern shores to eastern Queensland. It may occur in large numbers on rocky shores, where it feeds on algae and detritus.

Pheasant Shell *Phasianella australis* 40–60mm

This is one of southern Australia's most beautiful larger shells. The shiny shell is long, thin and turban-shaped, with eight smooth, rounded whorls. It has a high pointed spire. The shell pattern is very variable, richly marked with lines and patterns of delicate tints. The most frequent colours are pink, rose, cream, brown and red. The white calcareous operculum is oval-shaped and solid, pointed at one end. The umbilicus is sealed. This species ranges from Victoria across the southern shores to Geraldton in WA. It is found at and below low-tide levels on algae and seagrasses, on open, low- to medium-energy shores and in bays.

Swollen Pheasant Shell *Phasianella ventricosa* 30–40mm

This is a very beautifully marked shell with a great diversity of colour patterns. The shell is large, thin, turban-shaped and pointed at one end. Its spire height is 1.5 times its width. The shell is highly polished and very smooth, with no sculpture except for a suture around the whorl.

The aperture is oval with a heavy calcareous operculum. Some are unicoloured, while others are zebra-striped. This species ranges from NSW, around the southern shores to Geraldton in WA. It occurs in regions where sand and rocks meet on protected shores, usually with a strong growth of algae, on which it feeds.

Common Warrener *Turbo undulata* 70mm

This medium-sized mollusc has a wide, round, turban-shaped shell. The whorls are rounded, with low spiral ridges and deep sutures. The shell is dark bluish-green, mottled with white zigzag streaks. The living creature's shell may be covered with a brown epidermis. The aperture is circular, covered by a thick, white calcareous operculum, marked on the underside with a flat spiral. This species ranges from NSW around the southern shores to Geraldton in WA, including Tasmania. It is found at mid- to low-tide levels in rock pools and crevices on medium- to high-energy shores. It grazes on algae. The small **Bonnet Limpet** (see page 107) is sometimes found attached near the aperture to Common Warreners.

Turban Shell *Turbo torquata* 95–110mm

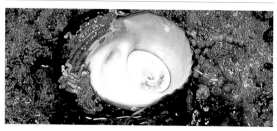

This shell is large, solid and orb-shaped, twice as wide as it is high. The sculpture is of oblique, close, longitudinal, thin plate-like striations and bold, concentric, coarse ridges. The early whorls are keeled. The circular operculum is covered with fine prickles and raised spiral ridges around a central hollow. The exterior is usually greyish-green but some are sand-coloured. Juveniles have orange mottling. Inside the aperture and the columella is white and nacreous. This species ranges from NSW around the southern shores to Geraldton in WA. It is rare in Victoria and Tasmania. It occurs at low-tide levels and below to 20m. It is found in deep pools or sheltered crevices. A heavily keeled, orange-coloured form, *T. torquata whitleyi* (bottom photo), exists in WA. Intermediate forms occur along the southern shoreline.

Military Turban *Turbo imperialis* 80mm

A very large, solid and heavy turban shell from eastern Australia, it is also known as *Turbo militaris*. The whorls are rounded and smooth but not polished. Some shells have a few pronounced spines. The aperture is large and oval. The outside surface of the white operculum may be sculptured with many small bumps. The shell is greenish and silver, with orange and brown markings. Inside the shell and the columella is nacreous. This species ranges from northern Queensland to southern NSW, occurring at the lowest tide levels on rocky ocean shores at the level of Cunjevoi and below, in gutters and in deep pools. It feeds on algae. Over the past 20 years, it has become more common in NSW.

Beautiful Turban *Turbo pulcher* 80mm

The solid, turban-shaped shell has a reasonably high spire. The sculpture is of rounded whorls, with spiral ribs crossed by close, thin, low, scaled ridges or lamellae. The umbilicus is sealed. The operculum is circular and thick, with blunt tubercles covering the convex outer surface. The exterior colour is fawn, with brown axial, wavy stripes and some orange and green mottling. The operculum outer surface, aperture and columella are white. The distribution is limited to WA, ranging from Esperance to Shark Bay. It occurs at low-tide level and below, in gutters and in pools, on reefs and platforms, where it grazes on algae. It is a distinctive temperate representative of a mainly tropical genus.

Turbo *Turbo cinereus* 35–40mm

The shell is thick and globe-shaped, with a large body whorl and domed spire. The whorls are rounded, without shoulders. The sculpture is of finely noduled spiral cords and faint axial striations. The aperture is round and the operculum is domed and sculptured with fine granules. The outer lip has a sharp edge. The columella is wide and flat with an outward-flaring spout-like projection. The external shell colour is cream, fawn or grey, with brown or green spots or blotches on the ribs. The operculum is white, with a dark green crescent mark on the outer margin. This species ranges from North West Cape in WA across the northern shores to Queensland. It occurs high on sand and shell grit beaches, sheltering among rocks.

Sand Creeper *Clypeomorus petrosa* 25–30mm

The tapering shell has a heavily noduled, strong spiral sculpture and an inflated body and last whorls. The sculpture is of eight or nine noduled spiral cords and numerous spiral threads on the body whorl as well as three nodular spiral cords and numerous threads on the spire whorls. It has an oblique aperture, with a backward-curving siphonal canal. The outer lip is thin and wavy. The shell is brown, yellow, white or cream, with white-tipped nodules and dark brown or black nodes, which create a spotted or banded appearance. This species ranges from Torres Strait to northern NSW. It occurs at mid- to low-tide levels and below, on sand or coral substrates, among algae and seagrasses.

Tent Shell *Australium tentoriiforme* 30–50mm

The shell is conical, bell-tent in shape, with a flattened base. Side on, the silhouette is almost a triangle. The mouth opening at the base is very angled (oblique). The white operculum is small and smooth, with one rib. The umbilicus is covered. The shell has a rich nacre finish, with a tint of purple. This species ranges from

south-eastern Queensland south into Victoria. It occurs at mid-tide levels and below, on rocky ocean shores, usually in pools and gutters. Although beautiful, it does not match its Western Australian relatives, where the beautiful vibrant blue colouring has caused western shells to be sought-after for jewellery.

Pyramid Trochus *Tectus pyramis* 60–80mm

This high-spired gastropod is easily identified by its perfect cone-like shape, colour and angled striations. A solid, conical shell with flat sides and a sharply angled margin to the flat base. The height and width are almost equal. The smooth sculpture has some growth lines crossed by oblique axial striations and weak nodules

near the sutures. The operculum is circular. The exterior colour is grey, green, cream or pink and the base white, green or light blue. It is nacreous beneath the periostracum. This species ranges from Rottnest Island in WA, across the northern shores to eastern Queensland. It occurs in large numbers on coral reefs and rocky shores and feeds on short, fine algae.

Black Nerite *Nerita atramentosa* 20–25mm

A distinctive black, globe-shaped shell with a flat spire and large body whorl. Its surface is smooth or marked with fine spiral striations caused by irregular growth lines. The aperture is large and semi-circular with one or two teeth at the side. The aperture and columella are white. The black or grey operculum is calcareous and granular outside. This species ranges from southern Queensland around southern Australia to North West Cape in WA. It is found abundantly at mid- to high-tide levels on and under rocks, in crevices and around the edges of rock pools on shores with low to moderate wave action. It feeds by scraping algae from rocks.

Changeable Nerite *Nerita chamaeleon* 20mm

This variable nerite has a broad, turban-shaped shell with a low spire. It is sculptured with rough spiral ribs, often with secondary ribs between. The outer lip has a sharp edge with weak teeth. The columellar deck or platform is narrow, sculptured with weak pustule-bumps and striations and two to four centrally placed marginal teeth. It has a very variable coloration, hence its species name. The exterior may be an evenly coloured yellow, orange, red, grey, white or black or may be banded or spotted with grey, purple or black. The interior and columellar deck are white and the finely granular operculum is grey. This species ranges from North West Cape in WA, across the northern shores to southern Queensland. It occurs fairly high on intertidal shores and protected reefs.

Ribbed Nerite *Nerita costata* 20–35mm

A turban-shaped shell with a high spire, sculptured with 12–15 broad, spiral ribs. The outer lip edge is sharp and grooved. The inner lip has strong teeth, with one large one at the posterior end. The columellar deck is sculptured with strong pustule-like bumps at the anterior end, and has cross striations at the posterior end and four or five large teeth at the margin. The grey or green operculum has very fine granules. The shell exterior is dull black, with white to yellow between the ribs. Its range is limited to eastern Queensland. It occurs at high-tide levels and below, exposed to the sun for long periods. The tight-fitting operculum prevents water loss. It seems to be less common than other nerite species.

Scaled Nerite *Nerita squamulata* 30mm

This shell has a flattened globe shape with its width greater than its height, producing a low spire. Its sculpture is of scaly spiral cords and axial threads. The axial growth lines are distinct. The outer lip of the aperture is flaring, with small bumps inside. The

columellar platform is concave, sculptured with nodules and has four to six small bumps at the margin. The green-tinged operculum has fine granules. The exterior colour is brown, orange of grey, with darker spotting and spiral bands. Inside the shell is pale green to white. This species ranges from North West Cape in WA, across the northern shores to northern Queensland. It is found high on sandy shores, sheltering beside rocks.

Wave-marked Nerite *Nerita undata* 25–35mm

This thick shell is more turban-shaped than other nerites and is sculptured with spiral riblets. There are many teeth on the inner edge of the outer lip. Three or more larger teeth are found on the inner margin of the columella. The colour is variable and may be yellow, buff, grey or black, with grey, green or black patches or spots. The white aperture area is often tinged yellow. This species ranges from Geraldton in WA, across the northern shores to eastern Queensland. It occurs high on mud and rocky shores in areas with brackish, muddy, water. The heavy operculum has a securing peg on its inner surface. When closed tight across the aperture, it can retain sufficient water to survive for days before being submerged again.

Striped-mouth Conniwink *Bembicium nanum* 8–10mm

A common, cone-shaped, univalve mollusc, with oblique brown and white bands on its last whorl. The shell is wider than high, with a cone-shaped, flat base. There are prominent bandings and sculpture on base whorl consisting of eight low concentric ridges. Other whorls are smooth or with small nodules. The shell is often eroded. The base colour is grey or white, with oblique brown and white bands, dominant on the last whorl. The interior is shiny, with dark brown stripes on the outer edge. The operculum is yellow-brown and horny. This species ranges from southern Queensland, around the southern shores to south-western WA. It occurs commonly from mid- to high-tide levels on exposed rocks and shore platforms.

Dark-mouthed Conniwink *Bembicium melanostoma* 15–20mm

The shell is cone-shaped, wide and keeled on the base whorl. The sculpture is of spiral ridges or nodules. It is smaller and less strongly keeled and the base is speckled with brown, producing a darker outer lip than the **Gold-mouthed Conniwink** (see below). The mouth is oblique, with a thin outer lip. The operculum is horny. The shell colour is grey or brownish, often with darker grey or brown oblique stripes. The stripes are less prominent than the **Striped-mouth Conniwink** (see page 98). The interior is fawn to dark brown and shiny, with a striped edge. The columella is orange or fawn. This species ranges from NSW, around the southern shores to Fremantle in WA. It occurs in sheltered estuaries, inlets, bays, mangrove swamps or on mudflats.

Gold-mouthed Conniwink *Bembicium auratum* 15–20mm

The rugged nodules on the whorls and the yellow-brown base distinguish this conniwink. The shell is a flattened cone-shape, with an acute angle to the flat base. The sculpture consists of rugged, flat, overlapping spiral ribs on the whorls. The body whorl has a tuberculated keel. The aperture is oval with a horny operculum. The shell colour is pale yellow to greenish-brown with faint bluish-grey markings or wavy oblique stripes. The base is yellow-brown or gold. It has a dark chocolate interior and a golden-brown columella. This species ranges from southern Queensland to the Houtman Abrolhos in WA. It is found in estuaries in areas dominated by mangroves. Occasionally, it occurs with mangroves on the open coast.

Blue Australwink *Nodilittorina unifasciata* 10–15mm

A small, turban-shaped shell with five to seven rounded whorls. The whorls are marked with very fine spiral striations, while the largest body whorl is partly keeled. The base is slightly flattened. The exterior colour is greyish-blue with a brown apex. A dark band circles the middle of the body whorl. The oval aperture is brown with a white band near the base. The interior and flattened columella are brown. The thick operculum is chitinous. This species ranges from southern Queensland around the southern shores to North West Cape in WA. It is found at and above high-tide levels, often clustered in groups on exposed rocks, where it feed on lichens. As these grow in size, they migrate up the shore.

Checkered Australwink *Nodilittorina praetermissa* 10–15mm

A small, solid, greyish-white shell with brownish zigzag stripes and a white stripe at the base. It is turban-shaped, with the spire less high than the shell height. The whorls are rounded, with faint spiral striations. The shell interior is reddish-brown, while the columella is yellowish to white. The thin operculum is dark brown. This species ranges from southern NSW to east of Kangaroo Island in SA. It is found at and above high-tide levels on exposed rocks and rock faces. It feeds by scraping algae off rock surfaces. Juveniles are black and globe-shaped and occur at low-tide levels. As they become adults, they migrate to higher shore levels.

Western Noddiwink *Nodilittorina australis* 18–20mm

This globe-shaped, spiral shell has a high, pointed spire and rough, granular exterior. It is distinguished by its sculpture of fine spiral striations around the whorls and low longitudinal folds. The spire is less than half the length of the shell. The aperture is oval. It is a light grey base colour with white transverse bands and a brown to bluish tinge. The interior and columella are light violet to tan. This species ranges from Esperance to the northern Kimberley in WA. It occurs on exposed rocky shores, at high-tide levels and below. This common species tends to be solitary, rather than gregarious like related species. It is an algal feeder. Also known as *Littorina australis*.

Noduled Littorina *Nodilittorina nodosa* 18–20mm

The outline and aperture are diamond-shaped. There are two rows of whitish to reddish-brown nodules over a dark brown base colour on the spire and body whorls. There are four or five flattened body whorls. The spire is less than half the length of the shell. The aperture is dark brown with a narrow white band. This species ranges from Geraldton to the Kimberley in WA. It occurs on rocks across all tide levels up into the splash zone. Both *N. australis* and *N. nodosa* have the same distribution range, live in the same habitats and readily hybridise. Rosewater (1970) considers both forms to be valid species, not two forms of the one species.

Tubercled Noddiwink *Nodilittorina pyramidalis* 15–18mm

A small turban-shaped shell with characteristic evenly shaped tubercles, found singly or living in groups on rocks at and above high-tide levels on exposed surfaces, moistened only by spray mist. Sculpture consists of two spiral rows of centrally located nodules, with many fine ridges. The shell colour is light blue-grey with fawn nodules. The oval-shaped aperture is brown, with a pale brown band near the base. The shell interior is reddish-brown. The columella is calloused and curved, while the operculum is horny and thin. This species ranges from Fremantle in WA across tropical northern Australia and south to NSW.

Dark Littorina *Nodilittorina acutispira* 7mm

This very small, long, turban-shaped dark-coloured littorinid is easily overlooked. It has four to six rounded whorls and is sculptured with weak spiral bev-elled ridges and irregu-lar, coarse axial growth lines. The spire is more than half the length of the shell. The aperture is oval. The colour is vari-

able, ranging from light yellowish-brown to dark brown, with a wide spiral band of brown to grey encircling the body whorl and anterior two-thirds of the spire whorls. It is speckled on the body whorl with white spots. The outer lip has a broad white band. It is found on the coasts of southern Queensland and NSW and is com-mon in rock pools.

Scratched Littoraria *Littoraria scabra* 40–43mm

This large, well-camouflaged, high-spired, turban-shaped molusc is found on mangroves. It has six to nine well-rounded whorls and the sculpture is of 10–12 weak to strong spiral cords with shallow spiral striations between. The axial sculpture is of fine growth lines. The operculum is large and thin. The species colour pattern is variable, usually a mosaic of zigzag or axial brown blotches or no pattern. It ranges from Shark Bay in WA, across the northern shores to northern NSW. It occurs across the Indo-Pacific oceans, and ranges from South Africa to eastern Polynesia. It is found on the trunks and roots of mangroves, on the ground and on man-made structures. It is not common on shore rocks, except in areas without mangroves. It is ovoviviparous, hatching live young within its body and producing related, inbred populations.

Jointed Littorina *Littoraria articulata* 20mm

This shell is turban-shaped, bent to the side. The sides of the whorls and the base are rounded. The sculpture is of 20–33 flat ribs on the large body whorl, with shallow grooves between. The columella is wide and empty. The shell exterior is cream-yellow, grey or white, pat-

terned with dark dashes on the ribs, which may form axial stripes. Inside the shell and the columella are dark purple, occasionally pink or white, edged white. This species ranges from Exmouth Gulf in WA across the northern shores to Moreton Bay in Queensland. It occurs in mangrove forests, sometimes on rocks and pilings.

Undulated Littorina *Littoraria undulata* 20–24mm

This turban-shaped shell has five to nine rounded whorls sculptured with seven to ten spiral, bevelled ridges. The spire is less than half the shell length. On the body whorl, weaker secondary striations lie between primary ones. The entire surface is covered with microscopic, closely spaced, wavy spiral threads. The axial sculpture is of regular, oblique growth lines, which form a faint reticulated pattern. The base is not flattened. The aperture is oval. Coloration varies from mottled yellowish-grey to banded dark brown with zigzag brown axial lines. This species ranges from North West Cape in WA to NSW. It lives intertidally on rocky shores, forming clusters in rock crevices during the daylight hours and becoming active at night.

Furrowed Clusterwink *Planaxis sulcatus* 20–25mm

A medium-sized, dark brown to grey, thick, oval-conical shell, with or without a spiral structure. It is often covered with a strong, fibrous periostracum. The aperture is oval and notched at the base of the columella. The operculum is thin and horny. It is dark brown to grey with darker markings, forming a striped or spotted appearance. The tip is often eroded white. Inside the shell is white, with brown stripes following the spirals. This species ranges from WA across the northern shores to southern Queensland. It is found in large groups under boulders and rocks in the tidal zone. It is abundant on beach rock on the mainland and Great Barrier Reef Islands. It feeds on algae and detritus.

Screw Shells *Turritella terebra* 170mm

A solid, long shell with a rounded base. The 20–25 strongly rounded whorls are strongly sculptured with spiral ribs or keels. The smaller whorls are fawn or cream, grading to brown on the larger whorls. It lacks an anterior canal notch, so the aperture is entire and almost circular. The operculum is horny. This species ranges from North West Cape in WA across the northern shores to central Queensland. It normally occurs subtidally but extends into the tidal zone. It prefers soft substrates, usually mud. It feeds by gathering fine particles of organic detritus trapped in mucous sheets on the gills and sucking them into the mantle cavity.

Giant Creeper *Campanile symbolicum* 180–200mm

This distinctive spiral shell is large, solid, long and turret-shaped. It has many smooth whorls, with sinuous growth lines. It is often heavily eroded, giving it a fossilised appearance. The anterior canal is short, lying almost horizontal. The columella and outer lip

are smooth. The shell exterior is chalky white, while the interior is glossy white. This species has a limited range from Esperance to Geraldton in WA. It occurs in shallow water with a sandy substrate. On some shores, such as at Point Peron, fossilised shells of this species are found everywhere embedded in the rock. On some shores, dead, heavily eroded and fossil shells lie together washed up on beaches. The genus has a long fossil record but this is the only surviving species.

Telescope-shell Creeper *Telescopium telescopium* 110mm

A very distinctive, large, telescope-shaped shell found on northern Australian estuarine mudflats. The shell is large and conical. The sculpture is of numerous flat-sided whorls and spiral grooves. The base has concentric cords and a deep channel around a short, twisted, columellar pillar. The anterior siphonal canal is short. The aperture is oval. The thin outer lip is flared. The exterior is brown, with a thin, white, central line on each whorl. The interior is brown with a yellowish columella. This species ranges from Exmouth Gulf in WA to the coast of central Queensland. It is abundant on muddy shores up to high-tide level. It can remain exposed for long periods. A herbivorous and detrital feeder.

Hercules' Club Whelk *Pyrazus ebeninus* 90mm

This distinctive mollusc is found in countless numbers on estuarine mudflats and mangrove swamps. It has a large, elongate, turreted shell and rounded whorls, with a flared rounded aperture. The sculpture is of low, longitudinal ridges, becoming angular and noduled on the last two whorls, and irregular concentric ridges. The anterior canal is short and broad. The columella is broad, with a turned-back inner lip. The operculum is brown, horny, flat and rounded. The shell exterior is dull dark brown to grey. The interior is brown, becoming white toward the shiny lip, margined with dark brown. This species ranges from northern Queensland to Lakes Entrance in Victoria. It was first collected by the crew of the *Endeavour* in 1770.

Stromb Shell *Strombus urceus* 50–60mm

This is a highly variable Indo–Pacific mollusc, with a solid shell, a high spire and a flaring, thick outer lip. The sculpture is of thick, bumpy whorls crossed by cords near the aperture lip, which is square-shaped in the north Australian subspecies **S. u. orrae** (see picture above). The operculum is horny, lengthened and pointed. The exterior is cream, brown, white or greenish with darker spiral lines, bands or blotches. Inside is white, purple or black, merging to yellow, then white at the columella. The Australian sub-species ranges from North West Cape in WA, across the northern shores to the Gulf of Carpentaria. It occurs in groups on sand or mud substrates, at low-tide levels and below to 20m.

Bonnet Limpet *Hipponix conicus* 10–15mm

This bonnet-shaped limpet has the habit of living on the shells of large molluscs. Its shell is small, solid, conical, cap-shaped, with a nearly round base. The apex is toward the rear and points backwards, often overhanging the rear edge. The sculpture

is of numerous irregular, broad, flattish ribs, becoming wrinkled in older specimens. There is no operculum. The exterior is brown, with a white interior bordered with chocolate brown. It is found all around Australia, under boulders and stones at at low-tide levels and below. It is able to excavate a cavity into the shell of the host mollusc, where it feeds on the faecal pellets of its host.

Spengler's Rock Whelk *Cabestana spengleri* 100–150mm

This conical whelk has a large, very solid, long and strongly sculptured shell with pairs of brown-red lines between the spiral ridges in the grooves. It is sculptured by broad spiral ridges, with large nodules in the centre of the whorls and many fine cross ridges. Abrupt breaks in the body whorl indicate a long pause in the shell growth. The outer lip is swollen and the spiral ribs go beyond its edge. The exterior colour is yellowish-brown, with a white inner lip and columella. The live animal is covered with a thin, brown, hairy periostracum. This species ranges from southern Queensland to SA, including Tasmania and New Zealand. It occurs in crevices and rock pools at low-tide levels and below. A carnivorous mollusc, it eats Cunjevoi.

Yellow-tinted Cowrie *Cypraea flaveola* 30mm

This longish, oval-shaped cowrie has a flat base with calloused margins. Its sculpture is of strong, prominent ridges or 'teeth', with those on the outer lip extending almost to the margin. The base colour is white with brown blotches. The sides are white with

conspicuous dark brown spots. The top is fawn or olive-green, tinged with yellow, with circular white spots and a distinctive mantle line. This species ranges from North West Cape in WA across the northern shores to central NSW. It occurs at low-tide levels and below, on rocky and coral shores. During the day, it hides in crevices and under stones, but at night it emerges to feed. It has formerly been known as *C. labrolineata*.

Snake's Head Cowrie *Cypraea caputserpentis* 35–40mm

This is a beautifully formed and coloured cowrie. The top of the shell is brown, with numerous white spots, forming a mottled pattern, while the base and sides are chocolate brown, lighter on the ends. The shell is solid, with the upper surface indented or depressed, with strong bumps on the lip. Northern shells have a thickened margin, expanded to form a flat base, while southern forms lack a thickened margin. This species ranges from Albany in southern WA, around the northern shores and south to southern NSW. Cowries' high gloss, striking colours, patterns and attractive forms make them a most highly sought shell by collectors.

Scaly Thais *Thais turbinoides* 30mm

Has a solid, oval to biconic shaped shell, with a moderately tall spire, a wide aperture and distinctive scaly sculpture. It looks something like a scaly **Mulberry Whelk** (see page 114). Its sculpture is of strong, spiral, scaly cords overlying axial longitudinal ribs. Two on the body whorl are spiny. The outer lip is thickened, with six distinct 'teeth', sometimes paired. The columella is slightly flattened. The anterior siphon canal is short. The exterior is whitish to yellowish-grey, with brown spots at the joins between the ribs and cords. The columella and inner lip are brown. This species ranges across the NT and Queensland coasts. It is sometimes exposed at low tide and is a predatory carnivore.

Cart-rut Shell *Dicathais orbita* 60–80mm

This large carnivorous mollusc changes its form gradually over its distribution range across southern Australia. So much so that previous researchers gave these forms three different scientific names. In eastern Australia, its common name, Cart-rut Shell, describes its massive, deep, spiral ribs (see above). Across southern Australia, the shell is smoother, with much lower, irregular, spiral ribs (previously *D. textilosa*) (see below). In southern WA, the shell lacks the deep grooves and has nodules and tubercles (previously, *D. aegrota*) (see bottom). Interestingly, in some areas, two

quite distinct forms occur together.

It is a large, solid, oval-shaped shell, with a short, low spire. Its body whorl is very large and rounded. The mouth and operculum are oval. The columella is flattened. The siphonal canal is a short, broad notch. The exterior is cream to white, with a white aperture, tinged yellow to orange near the lip. The end of the columella is yellow. The operculum is dark brown and horny. This species ranges from southern Queensland, around the southern shores to Barrow Island

in WA. It is also found in New Zealand. A carnivore, it occurs singly or in small groups, in crevices and rock pools at mid- to low-tide levels and below, often in regions of very strong wave action.

Spined Thais *Thais echinata* 50mm

This sturdy, thick oval-shaped shell has prominent pointed nodules. The spire is moderately high, sculptured with four rows of pointed nodules and spiral fine threads. The siphonal canal is a notch but with a thickened, spiny fasciole, consisting of bands that indicate the growth of the siphonal notch. The aperture and columella are smooth. The external colour is creamy grey to fawn, while the interior and columella are glossy white. It may be heavily eroded. This species ranges from the Houtman Abrolhos in WA, around the northern shores to southern Queensland. This is a common predator of the intertidal and shallow sublittoral on rocky shores and coral reefs. It feeds on barnacles, bivalves and other molluscs.

Wendletrap *Opalia australis* 40mm

The elongated, slender shell has numerous whorls, sculptured by eight thick longitudinal ribs extending across the whorls but not all the way around the shell. Near the aperture, on the last whorl, is a thickened ridge around the shell, meeting the horizontal ribs at right angles. Between these ridges, the shell is microscopically marked with delicate concentric and radial markings. The aperture is small and rounded, with a flattened base. The horny operculum is pure white in colour. This species ranges from Sydney, around the southern shores to Fremantle in WA. It occurs under stones at the lowest tide levels, where it feeds on anemones. It can emit a violet fluid as a defence.

Lustrous Cronia *Cronia margariticola* 40mm

This shell is oval to biconic in shape with a dominant spiral sculpture of noduled whorls, each with a distinct shoulder. There are 10–13 axial ribs on each whorl, crossed by noduled, scaled cords. The outer lip of the aperture has five or six bumps. The columella has one to three small teeth at the anterior end. The shell colour is dark purple-brown to black. The columella and lip are violet to bluish. This species ranges from North West Cape across the northern shores to northern NSW. It occurs on rocky shores, usually in mud areas, in the intertidal zone.

Coarse Cronia *Cronia crassulnata* 35mm

The shell is oval to biconic. The sculpture is of noduled whorls with angled shoulders and six to eight distinct axial ribs crossed by numerous spiral fine-scaled cords. The outer lip has four or five internal denticles. The columella is smooth or may have two very small denticles at the anterior end. The external colour is uniformly brownish-black, with a lilac columella and lip. This species ranges from North West Cape in WA, across the northern shores to the Gulf of Carpentaria. This shell is similar to **Lustrous Cronia** (see above) but is more biconic, has fewer axial ribs and is less scaly, although the ranges of the two do overlap.

Wine-mouthed Lepsiella *Lepsiella vinosa* 15–20mm

This shell is small, solid, more-or-less oval-shaped, with a conical spire less than half its total length. The spire often has a distinct shoulder. The distinct, wide, angular whorls are crossed by spiral ribs and the whole surface is covered by fine, scaly, intricate, thin plates. The anterior canal is short. The shell exterior is greenish-cream to grey and interior is dark purple-brown. The nearly oval, thin aperture is white, cream or brown and the columella is brown-purple or white. This species ranges from NSW, around the southern shores to Cockburn Sound in WA. It is a common, active carnivore and occurs on and under rocks, among *Galeolaria* tubes, mussel beds or on barnacles. It ranges widely between the tide marks.

Flinder's Lepsiella *Lepsiella flindersi* 30mm

This is a medium-sized, solid, spiral shell with a large last body whorl. It has a rough sculpture of strong spiral ribs, seven on the largest whorl. Fine lamellae run across the ribs. The aperture is broad, oblique and long, two-thirds the length of the shell. The exterior colour is white to greenish-white, with a light brown operculum. Inside is brownish. The columella is white with a yellow edge. This species ranges from Victoria to Cockburn Sound in WA. It occurs on rocks and reefs at low-tide level and below to 10m. A carnivorous mollusc, it feeds on barnacles and mussels. It is larger and wider than **Wine-mouthed Lepsiella** (see above), and *L. reticulata* has more nodules, marked with dark spots.

113

Mulberry Whelk *Morula marginalba* 25–30mm

This is an easily identified shell with spiral rows of heavy, rounded nodules, providing a distinctive 'mulberry' appearance. It is more-or-less biconic. The low spire is just longer than the aperture length. The columella is smooth and fairly straight. Externally it is whitish-grey with very dark purple to black tubercles. The outer lip is yellowish and the interior is blue-white, with a white columella. This species

ranges from central Queensland to NSW. It is abundant at most levels of a rocky ocean shore, especially near limpets and barnacles, on which it preys. It is also common in estuaries, where it preys on oysters. It uses salivary gland acid to dissolve through a prey's limy shell.

Tulip or Spindle Shell *Peristernia incarnata* 30mm

The shell is long, solid and biconic to spindle-shaped, with a short and wide siphonal canal. Its sculpture is of thick, rounded, oblique axial ribs and strong spiral cords. The columella is bent, with one to three weak folds. The outer lip has small bumps. The shell's axial ribs are yellow or red-brown, with dark brown interspaces. Inside the shell is mauve or pink. This species ranges from Geraldton in WA, across the northern shores to northern NSW. On the shores of WA, this is a common intertidal species, but it seems to be rarer in Queensland.

Spotted Cominella *Cominella lineolata* 25–30mm

This shell is oval-biconic, with a moderately high spire. Its whorls are sculptured with low, broad, spiral riblets or may be smooth. The shoulder may have nodules. The aperture has 10–12 spiral ribs on the outer wall, with a short siphonal canal at the front. The columella is smooth. Externally it may be cream, light yellow-brown or grey and may be banded with black, dark brown, orange or fawn. Broken spiral ribs may form spots, speckles or blotches. This species ranges from NSW around the southern shores to southern WA. It occurs at mid-tide level and below to 5m, in pools and under rocks, often in sandy and silty locations. At breeding time, several hundred may lay eggs communally.

Ribbed Cominella *Cominella eburnea* 30–40mm

This is a solid, biconic, high-spired shell with distinctly angled whorls. It has a distinct shoulder with heavy nodules. The whorls are sculptured with low spiral cords and grooves. it has a narrow-oval, ridged aperture ending in a wide anteri-

or canal, and a sharp outer lip. The brown columella is smooth and the operculum is horny. The exterior is light yellow-brown with irregular brown to reddish-brown spots or blotches, all partly obscured by a periostracum. The aperture is light brown with a white interior. This species ranges from NSW, across the southern shores to Geraldton in WA. It occurs on sandbanks and in rock pools of semi-protected bays and inlets, where it replaces the **Spotted Cominella** (see above), an open coast species.

Anemone Cone Shell *Conus anemone* 40–50mm

This shell is conical, with short, concave sides, and a short, pointed spire of varying lengths. Some specimens are high and shouldered. There are many spiral striations on the body whorl, larger at front and grooved near the base. The aperture is long, almost the length of the last whorl. The outer lip is thin. The operculum is small, pointed and horny. The colour is extremely variable and may have a cream, brown or bluish base marked with streaks, blotches or bands of brown, orange, pink or purple. Living cone shells are covered with a thin yellow periostracum. The animal is red. This species ranges from central NSW, around the southern shores to Geraldton in WA. It occurs under and among stones, in crevices or in pools, at the lowest tide levels and below to 15m.

Cone Shell *Conus papilliferus* 40mm

This shell is an inverted cone with a low spire, a tiny erect apex and a very strongly angled shoulder. Its sculpture is of faint spiral striations or cords. The body whorl has slightly convex sides. The aperture is long and narrow, with the lips almost parallel. There is an anal notch at the shoulder, while the siphonal notch is fairly deep. The shell is covered with a thin, sometimes furry periostracum. The shell is whitish with blue-grey blotches, covered with irregular, axially arranged brown blotches and rows of alternating brown and white dots. Inside the shell is violet to brown. This species ranges from Bowen, north-east Queensland to Mallacoota in eastern Victoria. It is fairly common in shallow water, extending into the intertidal zone.

116

New Zealand Siphon Shell *Siphonaria zelandica* 15–25mm

This siphon shell is quite flat with a thick margin. A sculpture of 17 main ribs has two or three riblets between. The outer margin of the shell is irregular, with a conspicuous siphonal groove underneath. The shell colour is greenish-cream, with white rib peaks and brown flecks in the spaces. Inside the shell is glossy, coloured tan to yellow. The muscle scar is brown to orange. This species ranges from southern Queensland, around the southern shores to southwestern WA, excluding Tasmania but including New Zealand. It occurs in groups at mid- to high-tide levels on rock platforms of medium- to high-energy shores. Usually found below **Van Diemen's Siphon Shell** (see below).

Van Diemen's Siphon Shell *Siphonaria diemenensis* 15–28mm

A siphon shell with a dark brown base colour and white radiating ribs. The shell is oval and limpet-like, with a central apex, leaning slightly backwards. Its sculpture is of 40 strong, radiating ribs. There is great variation in the shells, depending upon the habitat. Underneath the shell, a siphonal canal runs from the apex to the shell margin on the right side. The interior of the shell is chestnut brown with white alternating radial bands and an orange apex, dark at the shell edge. The animal is various shades of yellow. This species ranges from NSW around the southern shores to WA, including Tasmania. It is gregarious and occurs across all of the tidal zones.

Denticulated Siphon Shell *Siphonaria denticulata* 35–40mm

A limpet-like siphon shell, with prominent white radiating ribs and a strong, scalloped margin. It has a prominent siphonal groove on the undersurface. The shell is flatter but stronger ribbed than the **Corded Siphon Shell** (see page 119). Its base colour is grey to buff, with prominent white ribs and light brown markings between. Inside the shell is dark brown with a white edge. The species occurs along NSW shores. Some references state a tropical and eastern distribution. It occurs over the whole tidal region on rock platforms and lives with the **Variegated Limpet** (see page 79) and the Corded Siphon Shell. It feeds on algae.

Blue Siphon Shell *Siphonaria tasmanica* 15–23mm

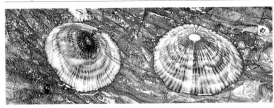

This shell is identified by its less prominent ribs and distinctive blue exterior. It is medium-sized, thin, oval and conical, with its apex toward the rear and left. The sculpture is of 40–50 flat radial ribs crossed by concentric growth striations. It is often eroded. The siphonal groove is indicated by a distinctive double rib. The exterior is bluish, with concentric brown bands that meet to form a brown apex. The shiny interior is a rich purplish to chocolate-brown and the spatula and siphonal canal are white. The animal is brown with a yellowish foot. It has a limited distribution between central Victoria and south-eastern SA. It occurs in sheltered areas and crevices at high-tide levels and below on medium- to high-energy coasts, usually on damp vertical rock faces. Also known as *Liriola tasmanica*.

Corded Siphon Shell *Siphonaria funiculata* 20–25mm

This is a conical, elevated, siphon shell with a sharp-pointed apex and numerous irregular, flat radial ribs with varying spaces between. The shell margin is crenulated and the siphonal groove is indistinct. The shell is brown with white ribs outside and shiny chocolate brown with a paler spatula inside. This species ranges from southern Queensland, around the southern shores to SA, including Tasmania. It occurs on rocky shores at high-tide level on rock faces and overhangs, generally lower than **Van Diemen's Siphon Shell** (see page 117). It is distinguished from Van Diemen's Siphon Shell by its finer ribs and brown interior. Found on many open coasts, it may be the dominant siphon shell on some south-eastern shores. It is also known as *S. virgulata*.

Onchidella *Onchidella patelloides* 25mm

This air-breathing, shell-less mollusc is small, oval and slug-like. It has a tall, thick leathery mantle covered with very small granules and large, scattered bumps. Generally it has a clean surface. The mantle border is scalloped. The head is small, with short conical tentacles and small eyes. It is green or yellowish-brown, with darker or lighter markings. This species ranges from NSW to northern Tasmania and also New Zealand. Locally abundant, it occurs at mid-tide level and below, usually under stones or under protective rock overhangs, often associated with *Galeolaria* encrustations and mussel beds. It is active nocturnally and on overcast days.

Bullina *Bullina lineata* 20–30mm

This is a beautiful mollusc with a small, solid, spirally grooved, white to cream shell, marked with a distinctive pattern of pink lines. It has a medium-sized spire and a large, wide, blue-margined foot that can be withdrawn into the shell and sealed with the operculum. Black eye-spots are located on mantle folds that lie in the front of the shell. The animal is almost translucent with a blue edge. This species ranges from Cowaramup in WA, around the northern shores to Bermagui in NSW. It occurs sporadically on sheltered sand and reefs at low-tidal levels, where it feeds on polychaete worms.

Sydney Sea Cow *Aplysia sydneyensis* 150mm

This is a medium-sized, elongated sea hare. It is a frequent visitor to the shore during summer, when it lays its long yellow egg strings near the low-tide level. Its smooth, thin, shield-shaped brown shell can be seen within the mantle flaps. Its colour is dark brown to almost black, with little or no mottling. If mottling does occur, it may be irregular shaped brown blotches, with brown to black streaks on the head. The pattern never forms rings. This species ranges from southern Queensland around the southern shores to south-western Australia. It occurs at low-tide level in pools, often under stones. If disturbed, it can swim through the water using 'swimming lobes'. It can release a purple fluid as camouflage.

Umbrella Shell *Umbraculum umbraculum* 140–150mm

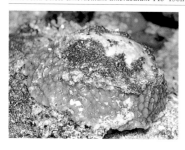

This unusual-looking, blob-shaped, 'wart'-covered mollusc has a medium limpet-shaped shell. Its large gill is at the front right side of the body. Jaws are absent but it has a many-toothed radula. It has a large foot and its head is peculiar in form. The shell is usually

covered by algae and encrusting animals. It has a thick, roughened periostracum. The Umbrella Shell has excellent disruptive camouflage, making it difficult to see in its habitat. Its colour is light brown on the warty areas, surrounded by darker brown. This species ranges from the Houtman Abrolhos in WA, across the northern shores to southern NSW. It occurs on moderately exposed reefs at the lowest tide levels and below to 200m.

Doriopsilla *Doriopsilla carneola* 60–70mm

This flattened, oval-shaped mollusc has a wide mantle and no shell. It has a firm body due to a dense mat of spicules within the skin. Its tail is short and rounded. Colour varies and may be dark reddish-brown, dull orange, pink, yellow or cream, with white markings. Other colour forms are dark red all over, red with a white foot or all white. The tentacles and gills are the same colour as the body. This species ranges from northern NSW around the southern shores to Cape Naturaliste in south-western Australia. It occurs under sponge-covered boulders at the lowest tide levels and below to 55m, or in rock pools in semi-protected areas.

Edible Mussel *Mytilus edulis planulatus* 50–120mm

This shell is wedge-shaped, broad and thickened, sharply pointed at the hinged end and extremely broad and rounded at the posterior end. Its sculpture is mostly smooth, except for concentric radial growth lines. The dark olive-brown periostracum is thick. The shell colour is bluish-black to dark brown. Juveniles are always brown. The interior is bluish-white. This species ranges from NSW around the southern shores to southern WA. It occurs on shores subjected to from low to moderate wave energy, usually in quiet, moist gutters down to 15m. It is also found on jetty piles in sheltered areas. It may be eaten raw or cooked, or used as fish bait.

Little Black Horse Mussel *Xenostrobus pulex* 15–30mm

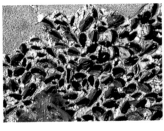

This small mussel is almost triangular in form. It has one edge straight, while the other edge has a distinct hump. The shell is long, inequilateral and flattened. The shell is mostly smooth, with a sculpture of fine concentric lines. The shell exterior is blue-black, covered by a shiny black periostracum. Inside the shell is slightly iridescent blue. This species ranges from NSW, around the southern shores to Yanchep in WA, and is also found in New Zealand. It is an extremely common species, living in large clusters where sand and rock meet on shores washed by medium- to high-energy waves. In some areas it also occurs on jetty piles.

122

Beaked Mussel *Brachidontes rostratus* 36–40mm

This long, equivale mussel has a distinctive umbo, which forms a sharp beak. Both the anterior and posterior ends are rounded. The sculpture is of fine radial striations. There are two or three teeth on the left valve and one to three teeth on the right valve. Several small bumps occur farther along the shell edge. The area near the umbo is often eroded. The exterior shell is purplish-black to nearly black. Inside is bluish-black to purple. Worn shells show more purple. This species ranges from southern NSW, around the southern shores to WA. It occurs in vast numbers on exposed rocky shores and in crevices below high-tide mark. On some shores, sheets of mussels cover large areas.

Rough-beaked Mussel *Brachidontes erosus* 60–70mm

This elongate bivalve mussel is narrow at the anterior end and wide at the posterior. Both valves are of equal size but are not symmetrical. It is similar to the **Beaked Mussel** (see above), but has less deep flattened ridges on the valves. There are several hinged teeth, the front ones being large, becoming smaller until they form crenulations. A periostracum covers the shell. The shell's base colour is brown, opal green or horn colour. This species ranges from San Remo in Victoria, to Albany in WA, including northern Tasmania. It occurs on sheltered rock and reefs, often embedded in spongy green algae, from mid-tide level and below to 4m. It is also found subtidally in mud bays attached to rocks. Also called *Hormomya erosa*.

123

Hairy Three-area Mussel *Trichomusculus barbatus* 10–12mm

This small, oblong-oval, partly haired mussel has three distinct areas to the shell. The area near the umbo is marked by fine radial ribs. The central area is smooth, except for very fine growth lines. The region near the opening is covered with long, distinctive bristles. All of the shell is covered with a shiny periostracum. The shell is greenish-yellow, while the periostracum is dark. Inside the shell is an almost iridescent white. This species ranges from NSW, around the southern shores to WA. It occurs at low-tide levels and below, under stones where sediment has accumulated or in gutters where there is sandy mud.

Razor Shell *Pinna bicolor* 400–500mm

A distinctive, very large, broad but thin, wedge- or fan-shaped bivalve. The two halves are sculptured with between 8–17 irregular ribs and concentric folds and striations. The shell is purplish-brown to horn colour with a distinctive nacreous sheen. A widespread species, it is found on most Australian shores, with the possible exception of Tasmania and

south-western Australia. Although not a rocky shore inhabitant, it may be found in the mud at the seaward face of many rocky or stony shores. It is often found in the company of others, with its sharp end embedded with a fibrous byssus some distance into the soft muddy bottom in areas of low to moderate water movement.

Rough Chama *Chama asperilla* 45mm

This oval-shaped bivalve has a distinctive sculpture of numerous backward-bending, arched spines. Its lower valve varies in depth and shape while the upper valve is convex. The sculpture on both valves consists of many closely positioned thin plates that grow into backward-curving, domed or arched bristly spines. The shell margin is mildly crenulated. The shell is white, with a purple tinge near the umbo. Inside the valves is white, sometimes with a purple margin. This species ranges from north-western Australia, across the northern shores to NSW. It occurs on rocky or coral shores and coastal platforms or attached to shell debris at low-tide level and below.

Common Mud Oyster *Ostrea angasi* 100–180mm

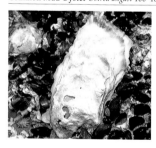

This bivalve, with a thick, heavy, rounded and compressed upper valve (shell) was an important food for Aborigines. The upper valve is flat to concave, sculptured with irregular, scaly, concentric growth lamellae, and often forms a fluted (wavy) shell margin. The lower valve (left) is flat to convex. The shell is ash-grey to off-white, usually darker toward

the hinge area. Inside the shell is white. This species ranges from NSW, around the southern shores to Fremantle in WA. It occurs at and below low-tide level, attached to stones and shells, or free-living in muddy areas. On southern Australian shores this oyster is marketed for eating.

Commercial Oyster *Saccostrea glomerata* 60–80mm

This oyster is harvested as a delicacy along eastern NSW. The shell is solid and irregularly shaped. The lower (left) valve attaches to rock or other solid objects. As it grows, it adopts the shape of its substrate and forms a cavity for the oyster viscera. The

lower valve is sculptured by several thick ribs crossed by concentric scales. The upper (right) valve is flattened, with a few scales near its outer edge. It fits into the shape of the left valve. One single, strong adductor muscle closes the shell. The shell exterior is bluish-white, while the inside is whitish with blue-black markings. This species ranges from southern Queensland to eastern Victoria. It occurs at mid-tide level, on shores influenced by fresh water. Also known as *S. cuccullata* and *S. commercialis*.

Spiked Oyster *Crassostrea echinata* 50–70mm

A large, variable oyster, with a long, rough, oval outline. Its lower valve is deep, with eight or nine deep ridges in exposed specimens and shallow ridges in protected ones. The upper valve is flattish, forming an upraised lip in older shells. The distinctive young have up to 24 strong spines extending vertically from the upper valve surface. In older shells these have been broken off. The upper valve is a bluish or purple-black with a slate-grey patch near the hinge. Eroded shells are all slate-grey, except for a black band inside the upraised rim. This species ranges from Thursday Island to Gladstone in Queensland and may extend through the Indonesian Archipelago to Malaysia. This is an intertidal oyster found on rocks and mangrove roots.

Codakia *Codakia rugifera* 50mm

This is a beautifully sculptured large bivalve with equal-sized, thick valves, which are inequilateral. The sculpture consists of about 30 coarse radial ribs, crossed by narrow concentric striations, which give it a rough appearance. It is white both inside and out. This species ranges from central NSW around the southern shores to SA. It occurs at the very lowest tide-levels and below. Codakia are often found as dead, isolated or deeply eroded shells, filled with sand, buried deep in gravel or in sand at the low-water mark and below.

Pipi *Donax deltoides* 40–60mm

This is a large equal-valved bivalve from sandy ocean beaches, which is strong, triangular and wedge-shaped. Its sculpture is of numerous very fine radial striations. The outside colour is bluish-white, tinted with cream, brown, olive, pink, yellow or rose. The shell surface is covered with greenish-brown epidermis. The interior is purple-mauve, dark violet or a pink tinge. This species ranges from southern Queensland to SA. In NSW it is called a Pipi, in southern Australia it is called a Goolwa Cockle, and in Queensland, a Ugari. It is found on sandy shores between headlands and usually occurs a few centimetres below the sand surface, near the low-water level. It is greatly valued by fishermen as bait but is also sold for food as 'butter clams'.

Biscuit Seastar *Tosia australis* 20–45mm

This is an attractive pentagonal seastar with the plates at the ends of the arms being swollen or enlarged. There are normally six plates along each arm radius. Similar species have seven plates. The rest of the upper surface is covered with plates that form an interesting pattern. The

upper surface colour may be greenish-brown, with patches of red, pink, orange, cream, mauve, purple and black. The lower surface is cream or dark grey, with some darker areas. This species ranges from NSW around the southern shores to southern WA, excluding western Tasmania. It occurs in the low tidal zone and below to 10m, on rocky or sandy substrates. It feeds on molluscs, detritus, encrusting ascidians and bryozoans.

Wilson's Seastar *Nectria wilsoni* 100mm

A brightly coloured five-rayed seastar with long tapering arms and concave, granular, raised tabulae (tables), covered with many small, rounded granules. These tables are well spaced and restricted to the central body section, growing smaller away from the centre, merging into raised bumps on the arms, which grow smaller near the arm

tips. It is a bright reddish-orange, darker between the tables. This species ranges from Lakes Entrance in Victoria, across the southern shores to Beagle Island in WA, including Tasmania. It occurs on moderately exposed reef and seagrass flats at and below low-tide level down to 45m.

Small Green Seastar *Patiriella exigua* 25–30mm

 A small, pentagonal, greenish to bluish seastar with five short arms just protruding beyond the skirt. Its dorsal plates are not well defined. It has short spines all over its surface. This species ranges from northern NSW, around the southern shores to Port Lincoln in SA, including Tasmania. It is dark green to bluish dorsally, with a light colour ventrally. It occurs up to mid- and high-tide levels in the open and under rocks in areas of constant wave splash and in rock pools. It is often found where there is the brown algae, **Neptune's Necklace** (see page 26).

Common Eight-armed Seastar *Patiriella calcar* 35–60mm

 This moderately large, abundant, gregarious, eight-armed seastar is extremely beautiful and varied in colour. It normally has eight, clear-cut, short, tapering, pointed arms but sometimes seven- and nine-armed individuals are found. Their colours cover many of the spectrum, including white, grey, cream, orange, red, brown, green, blue, mauve and black, often mottled and varied. Underneath it is uniformly pale. This species ranges from Currumbin, southeastern Queensland, around the southern shores to the south coast of WA, including the western coast of Tasmania. It is restricted to the tidal region and just below and is abundant in shallow rock pools, in cracks and in deep pools. It feeds on algae, detritus, molluscs and dead flesh.

Six-armed Seastar *Patiriella gunnii* 25–40mm

A thin, flat-bodied seastar resembling a hexagon. It usually has six very short arms, although it can have five to eight. The short arms do not extend beyond the skirt. The colour pattern is quite varied. It is as colourful as the **Common Eight-armed Seastar** (see page 129), but is darker and more dull. Its colours include a range of greens and browns, orange, pink, red, blue, mauve, with a little yellow or white. This species ranges from Sydney, around Australia's southern shores to Dongarra in south-western WA. It occurs at low-tide levels and below to 30m, sheltering under rocks and in crevices, where it feeds on encrusting organisms.

Purple Seastar *Patiriella brevispina* 60–140mm

This is a large, dark crimson to purple six-armed seastar with a thick, domed body. It is similar in form to the **Six-armed Seastar** (see above) but much larger, with the arms being more distinct. Its upper colour is a uniform dark crimson or purple, with deep orange tube feet. It may have a patchy distribution, which

ranges from central NSW, around the southern shores to Dongarra, southern WA. It may be common in some localities but rare or nonexistent in others. It occurs under boulders and in pools at low-tide levels and below to 30m.

Spiny Seastar *Allostichaster polyplax* 30–40mm

This small, long-armed seastar is seldom symmetrical because it can divide into two by autotomy. It is rare to see the arms all the same length. It normally has eight arms but there may be six to nine. Several arms may be smaller than the others. It may be uniform in colour or mottled or banded but is usually a subdued greyish-brown. It may have shades or markings of brown, red, orange, cream or greenish-grey. This species ranges from Sydney, around the southern shores to Rottnest Island in WA, including Tasmania and New Zealand. It occurs in the low-tide region and below to 130m. It prefers shelter, so is usually found under rocks, in crevices or inside dead shells.

Eleven-armed Seastar *Coscinasterias calamaria* 250mm

This large, strikingly beautiful, bluish seastar has long arms of varying lengths. It normally has 11 arms but may have 7–14. There are bicoloured spines on the dorsal surface, blue at base and salmon pink at the tips. Rings of hydraulically operated tube feet are in parallel rows on the bottom and top of the arms. It is blue normally, with shades of brown, orange, red, cream, mauve, grey and white. This species ranges from Point Danger in Queensland, around the southern shores to Rottnest Island in WA, including Tasmania and Lord Howe Island. It occurs at low-tide levels and below, found under rocks or wandering over algae in pools. It can reproduce itself by self-division, as well as sexually.

Brittle Star *Ophionereis schayeri* 300mm

This Brittle Star is distinguished by its light grey disc and its long snake-like arms prominently banded with dark grey, light grey or white. This is the largest and most common brittle star on Australia's temperate shores. Its upper surface is covered with extremely small overlapping scales, which become larger near the disc edge. Small spinelets are near the mouth. The spines on its arms are relatively short. The disc is 25mm across, while the arms grow to 130mm. This species ranges from Port Stephens in NSW, around the southern shores to the Houtman Abrolhos in WA, except Tasmania's west coast. It occurs at low-water levels and below to 200m, under rocks.

Heart-shaped Urchin *Echinocardium cordatum* 45–60mm

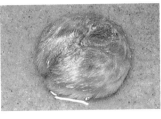

This urchin is not circular in outline but is a symmetrical heart shape. It is creamy white to light buff in colour. The tube feet are light brown and appear hairy. The perforated plates vary in size to create a five-leafed petal shape design. This pattern is

made up of twin rows of holes, through which hydraulic walking feet extend. Tube feet are also found on the undersurface. Underneath, the mouth is not central but lies toward the anterior end, which has a deep depression. This species ranges from Sydney, around the southern shores to WA, including Tasmania. It shelters in sand by excavating a slime-walled burrow, using its long spines with their flattened tips.

Common Sea Urchin *Heliocidaris erythrogramma* 90mm (test), 25mm (spines)

This is a common sea urchin, distinguished by its dark coloration and long, sharp spines. The test is flattened above and below, half as high as wide, covered with coarse tubercles. The primary spines are circular, long (25mm) and tapered to a point. The secondary spines have blunter tips. The test is light purple, green or creamy white. The primary spines are purple to dark olive-green, while the secondary spines are purple to dark green. The tube feet are pale pink. This species ranges from Port Stephens in NSW, around the southern shores to Shark Bay in WA. It occurs under stones and overhanging ledges in pools and gutters at low-tide level and below. It carves out a home hollow in rock.

Egg-shaped Sea Urchin *Amblypneustes ovum* 50–60mm

This globe-shaped sea urchin has dark primary spines, white secondary spines and orange-tipped tube feet. It has a creamy white to olive-green test. The test height is equal to or larger than its width, with a slight peak on the top surface, covered all

over with small tubercles. The greenish to black primary spines are short (5mm) and evenly spaced over the test. These primary spines are finely striated, slightly flattened and widened at the tips. The white secondary spines are slender but still grow to 5mm. This species ranges from central Victoria and Tasmania to Spencer Gulf in SA. It occurs at low-tide level and below to 70m. It is often found in shallow water and in rock pools, among algae.

Thickened Sea Urchin *Holopneustes pycnotilus* 60mm

This small, nearly globe-shaped sea urchin is distinguished by its brown or pale pink test, mostly transparent and colourless tube feet and bright lemon-coloured sucker tips. This genera has shorter and more delicate spines than other sea urchins. This sea urchin is confined to NSW between the Richmond River and Ulladulla. It occurs at low-tide levels and below to 8m. It prefers sheltered and moderately exposed rocky shores and reefs. It is easily overlooked if it is sheltering in a frond of algae. When dead, its interestingly sculptured bare test is often washed up on beaches after storms.

Pored Sea Urchin *Holopneustes porosissimus* 70mm

A distinctively coloured, globe-shaped sea urchin, with a greenish-grey test and mostly green spines, with bright red tips. The primary spines are short (2–3mm) and thick, in well-shaped rows, with blunt to knob-shaped ends. The secondary spines are smaller and not so ordered. The tube feet are purple. The very

wide pore zones are dark green and are arranged in irregular vertical series. The test is slightly wider than it is high, mildly flattened on the ventral side and densely covered with small tubercles. This species ranges from central Victoria across the southern shores to Fremantle in WA. It occurs at and below low-tide level, in shallow water, channels and in rock pools, usually attached to algae.

Black Holothurian *Mertensiothuria leucospilota* 400–500mm

This is a long, large, black but sometimes red-coloured, sausage-shaped holothurian of the tropical intertidal sandy shores and mud-flats. Its long, soft, pli-able, cylinder-shaped body is covered with soft bumps. Holothur-ians have a five-sided body plan, but it is hori-zontal, not vertical like other echinoderms. The mouth and 20 black tentacles occur at one end to test the environment and the anus at the other to expel unwanted material. This species ranges from Shark Bay in WA across the northern shores to southern Queensland and Lord Howe Island. The Cuvier's organs are abundant and conspicuous. If handled, these organs are read-ily ejected. This species was not used as edible bêche-de-mer as it is poisonous.

Chirodota *Chirodota gigas* 240–250mm

This is the largest of the south-eastern holothurians. It is easily recognised by its pink colour with numerous white spots. It is sausage-like, with a thin body wall and no tube feet. Its base colour is of various shades of pink, orange or red, with regular white spots overall. The white spots are clusters of tiny wheel-shaped spicules. This species ranges from central NSW, south to Victoria and most of Tasmania, with the exception of the far south coast. It is also found in New Zealand. It occurs on reefs under rocks buried in sediment, at low-tide levels and below to 10m and is occasionally found in rock pools at mid-tide level. It is sometimes found in large groups.

Cunjevoi *Pyura stolonifera* 80–150mm

Also called the 'sea-squirt', this Cunjevoi is squat and globular, with a thick, brown, leathery outer test, often obscured by algae. Fisherman use the red flesh as bait. It has a cylinder-shaped body with two siphons. Beating cilia bring water in through the branchial siphon. Inside, as water passes the pharynx, plankton is filtered out and moved to the stomach. Oxygen is absorbed and carbon dioxide removed, then the water passes out through the atrial siphon. This species ranges from southern Queensland around the southern shores to WA. It is found in large groupings low on the shore at and below low-tide level, attached to rock.

Another ascidian from southern waters is **P. sacciformis** (see lower picture). It is also found under boulders at the lowest tide levels. Ascidian are related to vertebrates, which include fish, amphibians, reptiles, birds and mammals. It is only during the Cunjevoi's juvenile tadpole-like larval stage that it possesses a notochord backbone. For only a few hours, it swims freely to a new site on which to settle. Here it attaches by the head, absorbs its tail, twists its mouth away from the rock surface and expands its body into the sessile adult ascidian form.

136

Crested Tern *Sterna bergii* 400–500mm

This large, handsome, common tern, is only slightly smaller than a Caspian Tern. It has a grey mantle and upper-wings, black shaggy crest on the head and the rest of the plumage is white. It has a large lemon-yellow bill. It is by far the most common tern around the Australian mainland and Tasmanian coasts. It may ascend rivers for some distance. It also ranges throughout the Indian Ocean, off South-East Asia and the western and central Pacific. It is often seen with other gulls and terns. It plunges for fish food at the water surface. It nests in small dense colonies on an island or cay where it lays two eggs in a sand scrape.

Silver Gull *Larus novaehollandiae* 400mm

This gull-shaped bird is so well known that identification is certain. The adult plumage is white with a grey back. The flight feathers have black tips with white 'mirrors'. It has a white eye, a red eye-ring and a scarlet bill and legs. It is a very common gull around the Australian coastal mainland and Tasmania, as well as New Zealand and New Caledonia. It is rare in northern Australia. It breeds in small to large colonies on islands, offshore or in lakes, dams and reservoirs, with from 1,000–4,000 nests per hectare. It is both territorial and migratory. It nests on the ground or in a dead tree in a lake, where it lays three or four eggs. It feeds on fish and other marine creatures, mainly as a scavenger.

137

Glossary

Acontia. Thread-like filaments armed with nematocysts.
Adductor muscles. Transverse muscles that draw valves together.
Ambulacra. Areas of body surface in which tube feet are situated.
Anterior. Situated forward, near the head end.
Apex. Initial end of shell of gastropods.
Aragonite. A form of calcium carbonate.
Ascidian. Solitary or colonial sea squirt of the phylum Chordata, enclosed in a soft, gelatinous test.
Atrial siphon. Exhalent siphon, expelling water.
Autotomy. Ability to cast off a body part, usually at a plane of weakness. Can be regrown.
Axial sculpture. Parallel to the axis, an imaginary line through the apex about which shells are coiled.
Biconical. Conical at each end.
Body-whorl. Largest whorl of a gastropod mollusc.
Branchial cavity. Channel between foot and girdle where gills are.
Byssus. Strong filaments, for attachment, secreted by foot gland.
Calcareous, calcite. Limy or shelly matter (calcium carbonate).
Carapace. Chitinous shield covering head and thorax of a crab.
Carnivorous, carnivore. Flesh-eating.
Carpus. Wrist or region between forearm and metacarpus in crabs.
Chelae. The pinching claw of a crab, with a movable and an immovable finger.
Cheliped. Claw-bearing appendage, terminating in chelae or pincer.
Chemosensory. Sensitive to chemical stimuli.
Chitin. Organic substance forming a horny cover of crustaceans.
Cilia. Hair-like projections that produce currents by waving.
Cirri. Feeding 'baskets' in barnacles.
Cloaca. Excretory cavity in some animals.
Columella. Central pillar or axis of coiling in gastropod molluscs.
Column. Body of sea anemone.
Commensal. Lives with another, but is not a parasite. Eats at the same table.
Crenulated, crenulations. Finely notched.
Cuvier's organs. Long, white, poisonous sticky threads ejected through the cloaca by a Holothurian when molested.
Dentate, denticulate. Toothed, small teeth or raised points.
Disc. Central part from which arms radiate, in some echinoderms.
Dorsal. Top.
Endemic. Native to a country or specific region.
Felted. Having a dense covering of short fine hair.
Fingers. The 'nippers' of the chelae, in crabs.
Flagellum. Lash-like process.
Fusiform. Spindle-shaped, in molluscs.
Gill. Respiratory organ in animals that obtains oxygen from water and releases carbon dioxide.
Girdle. Outer part of mantle, not covered by shell plates, in chitons.
Globose. Rounded like a globe.
Granulose. Covered with grains or tiny elevations.
Herbivore. Plant eating; in marine environments this is algae.
Hermaphrodite. Having both male and female reproductive organs.
Hirsute. Covered with hairs or bristles.
Holothurian. Sea cucumbers of the Phylum Echinodermata. Elon-

gated, soft and worm-like.

Interambulacra. Areas of test between ambulaca, in sea urchins.

Jugium. Longitudinal rib of the intermediate valve in a chiton.

Keel. Flattened ridge.

Lamellae, laminate. Thin plates or scales.

Larva. Self-contained embryo before it changes into adult form.

Lateral. Side.

Lateral plates. The side plates between carina and rostrum, in barnacles.

Laterals. Raised fan-like area on the side of chiton valves.

Mandible. Paired mouth appendages.

Mantle. Fleshy outer layer of body; secretes and protects shell.

Mantle cavity. Respiratory space between mantle and body.

Merus. The fourth segment of a crab's walking leg, which is attached to the carpus.

Monerans. Bacteria and cyanobacteria.

Nacreous, nacre. Having a pearly sheen.

Nematocyst. Cnidarian stinging cell.

Nocturnal. Active at night.

Nodule, nodulose, nodular. Small lump, knob or knot.

Notochord. Rod-like primitive backbone.

Omnivore. Generalist feeder, both herbivore and carnivore.

Operculum. Lid-closing aperture, in molluscs and barnacles.

Oral disc. Areas surrounding mouth, in anemones.

Orbital angle, or tooth. Angle at junction of eye orbit and lateral margin.

Ovoviviparous. Producing fully formed eggs that hatch inside the maternal body and are released later as live offspring.

Pallial. Pertaining to the mantle.

Parapodia. Lateral extensions of foot, in opisthobranch molluscs.

Pectinate. Like a comb.

Pentagonal. Having five sides and angles.

Periostracum. Thin coat of horny material on molluscs.

Pharynx. Cavity behind the mouth.

Pinnate. Divided in a feathery manner.

Plankton. Algae and animals drifting with surrounding water.

Pleopods. Small abdomenal limbs adapted for swimming and carrying eggs.

Polyp. A single zooid (individual) in a colony, in cnidarians.

Porcellaneous. Translucent, porcelain-like.

Primary spines. Longer spines, in sea urchins.

Proboscis. Long, retractable head extension with mouth at end.

Protoconch. The first, smallest whorls, which are the preserved larval shell, in gastropod molluscs.

Punctate. Surface sculptured with small depressions.

Pustule. Blister-like prominence.

Pyriform. Pear-shaped.

Radial symmetry. Equal proportion around a central point.

Radula. Tooth ribbon.

Regenerate. Regrow, renew or restore portion of body.

Reticulate. Network formation.

Rhinophores. Chemosensory-receptor tentacles or lobes on head.

Ribs. Raised lines in sculpture or ornamentation.

Rostrum. Beak-like projection of crab carapace between eyes.

Scalloped. Edged with semi-circular lobes.

Sculpture. Pattern on shell surface.

Secondary spines. Shorter spines, in sea urchins.

Sedentary. Rarely moving, not strictly confined to one place.

Sessile. Attached to the substrate.

Setae. Stiff, bristle-like structures in worms.

Shell. Calcareous covering secreted by mollusc mantle.

Siphon. Tube-like extension of the mantle edge to conduct water current for respiration and/or feeding, and for locomotion, as in molluscs.

Siphonal groove. A groove in the shell in which the siphon lies.

Spatula. Spoon-shaped.

Spicules. Needle-like bodies.

Spire. That part of shell (all whorls) above the aperture, in gastropod molluscs.

Striations. Narrow lines or grooves.

Sublittoral. Below low-tide level, marine.

Substrate. Surface on which an organism lives.

Suture. Line of junction of non-articulating parts; spiral line marking junction between whorls, in molluscs.

Teeth. Variety of sharp projections or bumps.

Telson. Hind part of abdomen, usually a sharp spike.

Tentacles. Flexible organs on head used as feelers, in molluscs.

Tessellated. Forming little geometric shapes, such as squares, triangles, etc.

Test. Shell or hard outer covering of echinoderms.

Thorax. Body region between head and abdomen.

Torsion. Mantle cavity twists to front of body during developmental growth, in molluscs.

Tube feet. Flexible tube-like stems used in locomotion, attachment and feeding.

Tubercle. Small rounded elevations on shell surface.

Tunic. Body wall of tunicates (ascidians).

Turbinate. Broadly conical spire, turban or top-shaped.

Umbilicus. Basal hollow in columella, in gastropod molluscs.

Umbo, umbone. Point or apex of bivalve shell above the hinge. It also marks the juvenile shell and sometimes the sculpture.

Valve. Shell segment of a chiton, or half the shell of a bivalve.

Varices. Prominent axial ridges on whorls, marks position of outer lip at successive stages of growth, in some gastropod molluscs.

Ventral. Lower or under-surface.

Verrucae. Blister or wart-like swellings on an anemone column.

Vesicle. A floating gas-filled bubble- or bladder-like structure.

Visceral mass. Internal organs.

Whorl. One turn of a spiral shell.

Further reading

Bennett, I. 1987. *W.J. Dakin's classic study, 'Australian Seashores'.* Angus & Robertson, Sydney.

Breidahl, H. 1997. *Australia's Southern Shores.* Lothian Books, Melbourne.

Edgar, G.J. 1997. *Australian Marine Life: The plants and animals of temperate waters.* Reed Books, Melbourne.

Hutchings, P. and Saenger, P. 1987. *Ecology of Mangroves.* University of Queensland Press, Brisbane.

Jones, D. and Morgan, G. 1994. *A Field Guide to Crustaceans of Australian Waters.* Reed, Sydney.

Macpherson, J.H. and Gabriel, C.J. 1962. *Marine Molluscs of Victoria.* Melbourne University Press and The National Museum of Victoria, Melbourne.

Marine Research Group of Victoria. 1984. *Coastal Invertebrates of Victoria: An atlas of selected species.* MRGV and Museum of Victoria, Melbourne.

Quinn, G.P., Wescott, G.C. and Synnot, R.N. 1992. *Life on Rocky Shores of South-Eastern Australia.* Victorian National Parks Association, Melbourne.

Rosewater, J. 1970. *The Family Littorinidae in the Asia-Pacific: Pt 1: The sub-family Littorininae: Indo-Pacific Mollusca.* V. 2(11), pp. 5–261.

Shepherd, S.A. and Thomas, I.M. 1982. *Marine Invertebrates of Southern Australia. Part I.* South Australian Government Printer, Adelaide.

Shepherd, S.A. and Thomas, I.M. 1989. *Marine Invertebrates of Southern Australia. Part II.* South Australian Government Printer, Adelaide.

Short, J.W. and Potter, D.G. 1987. *Shells of Queensland and the Great Barrier Reef: Marine gastropods.* Golden Press, Sydney.

Underwood, A.J. and Hutchings, P.A. 1987. *Australia's Seashores: The Australian Museum Environment Series.* Collins and The Australian Museum, Sydney.

Wells, F.E. and Bryce, C.W. 1988. *Seashells of Western Australia.* Western Australian Museum, Perth.

Wilson, B. 1993. *Australian Marine Shells, 1: Prosobranch gastropods.* Odyssey Publishing, Perth.

Wilson, B. 1993. *Australian Marine Shells, 2: Prosobranch gastropods: Neogastropods.* Odyssey Publishing, Perth.

Wilson, B.R. and Gillett, K. 1979. *A Field Guide to Australian Shells: Prosobranch gastropods.* A.H. & A.W. Reed, Sydney.

Womersley, H.B.S. 1984. *The Marine Benthic Flora of Southern Australia. Part I.* South Australian Government Printer, Adelaide.

Womersley, H.B.S. 1987. *The Marine Benthic Flora of Southern Australia. Part II.* South Australian Government Printer, Adelaide.

Various booklets produced by the Gould Society

Various booklets produced by the Victorian Institute of Marine Science

Index

Abalone, 14, 74
  Scarlet-rayed, 74
Acanthopleura gaimardi, 71
  A. gemmata, 70
  A. hirtosa, 71
Acmaeid limpets, 6
Actinae tenebrosa, 31
Algae, 7, 9, 11
  Brown, 7, 13, 23–27
  external features, 16
  Geniculate Coralline, 28
  Globe, 25
  grazers, 11
  Green, 7, 12, 20–22
  Iridescent, 28
  microscopic, 6, 11
  Red, 7, 13, 28–29
Allostichaster polyplax, 131
Amblychilepas nigrita, 76
Amblypneustes ovum, 133
Amphipods, 6
Amphiroa anceps, 28
Anemones, 7, 13, 31–33
  external features, 16
  Green, 32
  Sand, 32, 33
  Waratah, 31
Annelida, 13, 37–39
Anthozoa, 13, 31–36
Aplysia sydneyensis, 120
Arthropoda, 14
Ascidiacea, 15, 136
Ascidians, 12, 15, 136
Asteroidae, 15, 128–131
Atergatis integerrimus, 51
Australium tentoriiforme,
  95
Australwink
  Blue, 100
  Checkered, 100
Austrocochlea
  concamerata, 89
  A. constricta, 88
  A. odontis, 89
  A. porcata, 88
  A. rudis, 90
Aves, 15, 137
Balanus nigrescens, 44
  B. trigonus, 44
Barnacles, 6, 7, 14, 40–44
  Balanus, 7, 44
  external features, 16
  Giant Rock, 44
  high-shore, 6, 7
  Honeycomb, 42
  Malayan, 40
  reproduction, 12
  Rose-coloured, 42
  Rosette, 43
  Scaly, 43
  Six-plated, 40
  Surf, 44
  Wither's, 41
Barrier beach coasts, 4
Basalt shores, 5, 8
Behaviour patterns, 12
Bembicium auratum, 99
  B. melanostoma, 99
  B. nanum, 98
Biogeographic zones, 7–8
Birds, 15, 137
Bivalves, 14, 122–127
Bivalvia, 14, 122–127
Bluebottles, 19
Blue ringed octopus, 19
Blunt-tailed Sea Centipede,
  45
Boulder shores, 5, 11

Box jellyfish, 19
Brachidontes erosus, 123
  B. rostratus, 123
Bristleworms, 13, 37–39
Brittle stars, 15, 132
Brown Algae, 7, 13, 23–27
Bubble Weed, 21
Bullina, 120
Bullina lineata, 120
By-the-wind Sailer, 13, 34
Cabestana spengleri, 108
Campanile symbolicum, 105
Cart-rut Shell, 110
Catomerus polymerus, 40
Caulerpa, 22
Caulerpa filiformis, 22
Cellana conciliata, 80
  C. solida, 80
  C. tramoserica, 79
Chaetomorpha coliformis,
  21
  C. darwinii, 21
Chama asperilla, 125
Chama, Rough, 125
Chamaesipho tasmanica, 42
Champia compressa, 28
Chirodota, 135
Chirodota gigas, 135
Chiton pelliserpentis, 72
Chitons, 7, 14, 69–73
  Australian, 69
  Elongated, 69
  external features, 17
  Hairy, 71
  Jewelled, 70
  Mysterious, 73
  Snake-skin, 72
  Spiculed, 71
  Variegated Ischnochiton,
    70
  White Plaxifora, 72
  Yellow, 73
Chlorophyta, 12, 20–22
Chordata, 15, 136–137
Chthamalus antennatus, 40
  C. malayensis, 41
  C. withersii, 41
Cirripedia, 14, 40–44
Clams, 14
Classification, 12–15
Clusterwink, Furrowed, 104
Clypeomorus petrosa, 94
Clypidina rugosa, 77
Cnidaria, 12, 13, 31–36
Cnidopus verater, 33
Cockles, 14
Codium fragile, 21
Coenoloita variabilis, 46
Collisella mixta, 83
  C. onychitis, 83
Colpomenia sinuosa, 25
Cominella
  Ribbed, 115
  Spotted, 115
Cominella eburnea, 115
  C. lineolata, 115
Common Earshell
  (Abalone), 74
Cone Shell, 14, 116
  Anemone, 116
Conical Thalotia, 87
Conniwinks, 6, 7, 98–99
  Dark-mouthed, 99
  Gold-mouthed, 99
  Striped-mouthed, 98
Conus anemone, 116
  C. papilliferus, 116
Cool temperate zone, 8

Coral, 13, 35–36

Blue, 35
  Double-faced, 35
  Glomerate Soft, 36
Corallina officinalis, 29
Corallinaceae species, 29
Coralline Seaweed, 29
Coscinasterias calamaria,
  131
Cowrie, 109
  Yellow-tinted, 108
Crabs, 14, 46–68
  Bearded, 52
  Blue-swimmer, 49
  Brown Shawl, 51
  Burrowing Shore, 6, 57
  Canary-yellow Clawed
    Fiddler, 65
  Common Ghost, 60
  Compressed Fiddler, 64
  Dark Blue Soldier, 68
  decapods, 12, 14
  Distinctive Fiddler, 65
  external features, 17
  Fiddler, 64–67
  Flamed Fiddler, 64
  Grey Shore, 57
  Hairy Stone, 47
  Half-crabs, 14, 46
  Hermit, 14, 46
  Horn-eyed Ghost, 60
  Lemon-yellow Clawed
    Fiddler, 67
  Light Blue Soldier, 68
  Long-digit Uca, 65
  Metapograpsus, 59
  Mottled Shore, 54
  Mud Shore, 55
  Mudflat Sentinel, 62
  Notched Shore, 55
  Ocean Beach Surf, 6
  Ocypode, 6, 60–61
  Orange-clawed Fiddler,
    66
  Pea, 7
  Purple Shore, 53
  Red Bait, 58
  Red-fingered Marsh, 59
  Reef, 51
  reproduction, 12
  respiration, 11
  Sand Bubbler, 6, 63
  Seagrass Sentinel, 62
  Seaweed Decorator, 48
  Semaphore, 61
  shore, 7
  Smooth-handed, 52
  Smooth Pebble, 47
  Smooth Shore, 53
  Southern Sentinel, 63
  Sowrie, 58
  Spotted Smooth Shore,
    54
  Terrestrial Hermit, 46
  Thalamita, 49
  Three-pronged Spider, 48
  Tubercled Crab, 49
  Two-spined Burrowing
    Sand, 6, 50
  Variegated Shore, 57
  Western Ghost, 61
  Xanthidae, 51
Creepers
  Giant, 105
  Sand, 94
  Telescope-shell, 106

Crested Tern, 15, 137
Cronia
    Coarse, 112
    Lustrous, 112
Cronia crassulnata, 112
    C. margariticola, 112
Crustaceans, 14, 17
Cryptoplax mystica, 73
Cunjevoi, 6, 7, 136
Cyclograpsus audouinii, 53
    C. granulosus, 53
Cypraea caputserpentis, 109
    C. flaveola, 108
Cystophora torulosa, 27
Dangerous animals, 19
Decapods, 12, 14, 17, 46–68
Dendronephthya klunzigeri, 36
Desiccation, 10
Dicathais aegrota, 110
    D. orbita, 110
    D. textilosa, 110
Dictyota dichotoma, 24
Diodora, 76
Diodora lineata, 76
Dittosa laevis, 47
Doriopsilla, 121
Doriopsilla carneola, 121
Doubling Weed, 24
Durvillaea potatorum, 25
Eastern tropical zone, 7
Eastern warm temperate zone, 8
Echinocardium cordatum, 132
Echinodermata, 15, 128–135
Echinoderms, 12, 15, 128–135
Echinoidea, 15, 132–134
Ectocarpus, 23
Ectocarpus siliculosus, 23
Eklonia radiata, 26
Elephant Snail, 75
Encrusting Corallines, 29
Enteromorpha intestinalis, 20
Errantia, 13
Estuarine shore zonation, 6
Eunice, 37
Eunice aphroditois, 37
Eurythoe complanata, 37
Excretion, 12
False Ear Shell, 86
    Elongated, 86
    Rounded, 86
Fiddler Crabs, 64–67
Food, 11–12
Galeolaria, 6, 7, 38, 39, 77
Galeolaria caespitosa, 38
Gastropoda, 14, 74–121
Gastropods, 14, 17, 74–121
Giant Creeper, 105
Goniophora lobata 36
Granata inbricata, 86
Granite shores, 5, 8
Green Algae, 7, 12, 20–22
Green Bait Weed, 20
Green Sea Velvet, 21
Half-crab, 14, 46
Halicarcinus ovatus, 48
Halimeda, 22
Halimeda cuneata, 22
Haliotis coccoradiata, 74
    H. rubra, 74
Helice leachi, 57
Helicon chapmani, 78
Heliocidaris erythrogram-ma, 133
Helipora coerulea, 35

Heloecius cordiformis, 61
Helograpsus haswellianus, 55
Hemiplax latifrons, 63
Hermit crab, 14, 46
Heteractis malu, 33
Heteropilumnus fimbriatus, 52
Hipponix conicus, 107
Holopneustes porosissimus, 134
    H. pycnotilus, 134
Holothurians, 7, 15, 135
    Black, 135
Holothuroidea, 15, 135
Hormosira banksii, 26
Hydroids, 13, 34
Idanthyrsus, 38
Idanthyrsus pennatus, 38
Intertidal organisms, 6, 7, 10, 11
Ischnochiton australis, 69
    I. elongatus, 69
    I. versicolor, 70
Isopods, 6
Kelp, 12, 13
    Bull, 25
    Leather, 26
Land snails, 14
Larus novaehollandiae, 137
Lepidonotus melanogram-mus, 39
Lepisella
    Flinder's, 113
    Wine-mouthed, 113
Lepisella findersi, 113
    L. reticulata, 113
    L. vinosa, 113
Leptograpsus octodentatus, 6, 57
    L. variegatus, 56
Ligia australiensis, 6, 45
Limestone shores, 5, 8
Limpets, 7, 14, 76–85
    acmaeid, 6
    Banded, 83
    Black Keyhole, 76
    Bonnet, 107
    Chapman's, 78
    Cryptic, 82
    Diodora, 76
    False, 77
    Flamed, 85
    Giant, 78
    Granulated, 83
    Lateral-striped, 81
    May's Beetle, 84
    Orange-edged, 80
    Patelloid, 6, 81–82
    Petterd's, 85
    Rainbow, 80
    Scaly, 77
    Tall, 84
    Tall-ribbed, 81
    Variegated, 79
Littoraria articulata, 103
    L. scabra, 103
    L. undulata, 103
Littorina, Scratched, 103
Littorina, 4
    Dark, 102
    Jointed, 103
    Noduled, 101
    Undulated, 104
Littorinids, 7
Lobsters, 14
Lomis hirta, 44
Long Digit Uca, 65
Macrophthalmus crassipes, 62
    M. latifrons, 63

M. setosus, 62
Mainland beach coasts, 4
Malacostraca, 14, 45–68
Mangroves, 4, 11
Marine Slater, 45
Matuta planipes, 6, 50
Mertensiothuria leucospi-lota, 135
Metamorphic rock shores, 5, 8
Metapograpsus, 59
Metapograpsus frontalis, 59
    M. latifrons, 59
Mictyris longicarpus, 68
    M. platycheles, 68
Molluscs, 10, 14, 69–127
    chitons, 7, 14, 69–73
    external features, 17
    predatory, 11
    reproduction, 12
    respiration, 11
    semi-mobile, 6
    two-shelled aquatic, 14
Monodonta labio, 90
Morula marginalba, 114
Mussels, 14, 122–124
    Beaked, 123
    Edible, 122
    Hairy Three-area, 124
    Little Black Horse, 122
    Rough-beaked, 123
Mytilus edulis planulatus, 122
Naxia tumida, 48
Nectocarcinus tuberculosus, 49
Nectria wilsoni, 128
Nematocysts, 13
Neptune's Necklace, 26
Nerita atramentosa, 96
    N. chamaeleon, 96
    N. costata, 97
    N. squamulata, 97
    N. undata, 98
Nerites, 6, 11, 96–98
    Black, 96
    Changeable, 96
    Ribbed, 97
    Scaled, 97
    Wave-marked, 98
Noddiwinks
    Tuberculed, 102
    Western, 101
Nodilittorina, 4
    N. acutispira, 102
    N. australis, 101
    N. nodosa, 101
    N. praetermissa, 100
    N. pyramidalis, 102
    N. unifasciata, 100
Notoacmea alta, 84
    N. flammea, 85
    N. mayi, 84
    N. petterdi, 85
Ocypode ceratopthalma, 60
    O. convexa, 6, 61
    O. cordiformis, 61
    O. cordimana, 6, 60
Ocypode crabs, 6, 60–61
Onchidella, 119
Onchidella patelloides, 119
Onithochiton quercinus, 73
Opalia australis, 111
Ophionereidae, 15, 132
Ophionereis schayeri, 132
Ostrea angasi, 125
Oulactis macmurrichi, 32
    O. muscosa, 32
Ovalipes australiensis, 6
Oysters, 6, 14
    Common Mud, 125

Ozius truncatus, 51
Padina, 24
Padina pavonea, 24
Paragrapsus gaimardii, 54
  P. laevis, 54
  P. quadridentatus, 55
Paridolea munda, 45
Patella laticostata, 78
  P. peroni, 77
Patelloida alticostata, 81
  P. cryptalirata, 82
  P. latistrigata, 81
  P. saccharina stella, 82
Patiriella brevispina, 130
  P. calcar, 129
  P. exigua, 129
  P. gunnii, 130
Peristernia incarnata, 114
Petrolisthes elongatus, 46
Phaeophyta, 13, 23–27
Phascolosoma annulatum, 39
  P. noduliferum, 39
Phasianella australis, 91
  P. ventricosa, 91
Pheasant Shell, 91
  Swollen, 91
Philyra laevis, 47
Phlyctenanthus australis, 31
Phyllospora comosa, 27
Phylum Annelida, 13, 37–39
Phylum Arthropoda, 14
Phylum Chlorophyta, 12, 20–22
Phylum Chordata, 15, 136–137
Phylum Cnidaria, 13, 31–36
Phylum Echinodermata, 15
Phylum Mollusca, 14, 69–127
Phylum Phaeophyta, 13, 23–27
Phylum Porifera, 13, 30
Phylum Rhodophyta, 13, 28–29
Phylum Sipuncula, 13
Pill bugs, 14, 45
Pilumnopeus serratifrons, 52
Pinna bicolor, 124
Pinnotheres hickmani, 67
Pipis, 6
Plagusia chabrus, 58
  P. glabra, 58
Planaxis sulcatus, 104
Plankton, 11, 12
Plaxiphora albida, 72
Polychaeta, 13, 37–39
Polychaete worms, 6, 7, 13, 37–39
Polyplacophora, 14, 69–73
Porifera, 13, 30
Portunus pelagicus, 50
Prawns, 14
Protochordates, 15, 136
Protopalythoa australiensis, 34
Pyrazus ebeninus, 106
Pyura sacciformis, 136
  P. stolonifera, 136
Razor Shell, 124
Red Algae, 7, 13, 28–29
Reproduction, 12
Respiration, 11
Rhodophyta, 13, 28–29
Rocky shores, 4–5, 8
  conservation code, 19
  zonation, 5–7
Salinity, 11
Sand Creeper, 94

Sand-hoppers, 6
Sandstone shores, 5
Sandy shore zonation, 5–6
Sausage Weed, 23
Scallops, 14
Scopimera inflata, 6, 63
Screw Shells, 105
Scutus, 75
Scutus antipodes, 75
  S. granulatus, 75
  S. olonguis, 75
  S. unguis, 75
Sea anemones, 7, 13, 16, 31–33
Sea Cow, Sydney, 120
Sea cucumbers, 15, 135
Sea hares, 14, 120–121
Sea jellies, 19
Sea lettuce, 20
Sea snails, 14
Sea snakes, 19
Sea stars, 7, 15, 128–131
  Biscuit, 128
  Brittle, 132
  Common Eight-armed, 129
  Eleven-armed, 131
  Purple, 130
  Six-armed, 130
  Small Green, 129
  Spiny, 131
  Wilson's, 128
Sea urchins, 7, 15, 132–134
  Common, 133
  Egg-shaped, 133
  external features, 16
  Heart-shaped, 132
  Pored, 134
  Thickened, 134
Seaweed, 12
  Brown, 27
  Coralline, 29
  Sedentaria, 13
Sesarma erythrodactyla, 59
Sessile organisms, 6
Shipworms, 14
Shrimps, 14
Silver Gull, 15, 137
Siphon shells, 6, 7, 117–119
  Blue, 118
  Corded, 119
  Denticulated, 118
  New Zealand, 117
  Van Diemen's, 117
Siphonaria denticulata, 118
  S. diemenensis, 117
  S. funiculata, 119
  S. tasmanica, 118
  S. zelandica, 117
Siphonids, 7
Sipuncula, 13
Slaters, Marine, 14, 45
Slugs, 14
Snails, 14
  Elephant, 75
Soldier Crabs, 68
Spindle Shell, 114
Splachnidium rugosum, 23
Sponges, 7, 13, 30
Sterna bergii, 137
Stomatella impertusa, 86
Strap Weed, 27
Stromb Shell, 107
Strombus urceus, 107
Tectus pyramis, 95
Telescopium telescopium, 106
Tent Shell, 95
Tesserropora rosea, 42
Tetraclitella purpurascens, 43

T. squamosa, 43
Thais
  Scaly, 109
  Spined, 111
Thais echinata, 111
  T. turbinoides, 109
Thalamita crenata, 49
Thalotia conica, 87
Tidal plain coasts, 4
Top shells, 6, 7, 88–90
  Checkered, 89
  Ribbed, 88
  Smooth, 90
  Wavy, 89
  Zebra, 88
Tosia australis, 128
Tritons, 7
Trochus
  Lined, 87
  Pyramid, 95
Trochus lineatus, 87
Tulip Shell, 114
Turbans, 7, 92–94
  Beautiful, 93
  Common Warrener, 92
  Military, 93
Turbinaria bifrons, 35
Turbo, 94
Turbo cinereus, 94
  T. inperialis, 93
  T. pulcher, 93
  T. torquata, 92
  T. undulata, 92
Turritella terebra, 105
Uca coarctata, 64
  U. flammula, 64
  U. longidigita, 65
  U. mjobergi, 66
  U. perplexa, 67
  U. signata, 65
  U. vomeris, 66
Ulva species, 20
Umbraculum umbraculum, 121
Umbrella Shell, 121
Variegated Ischnochiton, 70
Velella velella, 13, 34
Vertebrates, 15, 137
Warrener, Common, 92
Wave energy, 4, 10
Wendletrap, 111
Western tropical zone, 8
Western warm temperate zone, 8
Whelks, 7, 14
  Hercules' Club, 106
  Mud, 6
  Mulberry, 114
Woodlice, 14, 45
Worms, 13, 37–39
  Bristle, 13, 37–39
  Errantia, 13
  external features, 16
  Spengler's Rock, 108
  Fire, 37
  Galeolaria, 6, 7, 38
  Idanthyrsus, 38
  Peanut, 13, 39
  Polychaete, 6, 7, 13, 37–39
  Scale, 39
  Sedentaria, 13
  segmented, 13, 37–39
  Shipworms, 14
  tube, 6
Xenostrobus pulex, 122
Yabbies, 14
Zoanthid, 34
Zonation, 5–7

144